ALCATRAZ ISLAND
MEMORIES

by
Donald J. Hurley

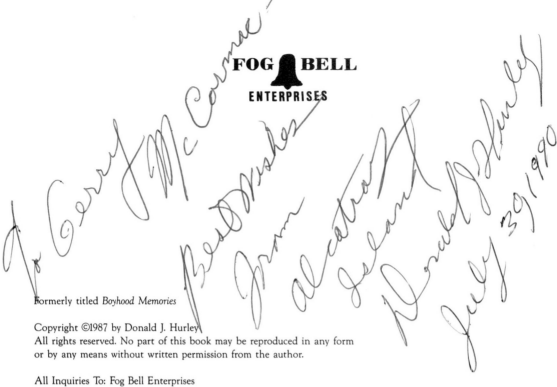

FOG BELL ENTERPRISES

Formerly titled *Boyhood Memories*

All Inquiries To: Fog Bell Enterprises
P.O. Box 1376
Sonoma, CA 95476

Printed in the United States of America

Revised Edition—Second Printing, June 1988
        Third Printing, January 1989
        Fourth Printing, June 1989
        Fifth Printing, May 1990

Library of Congress Catalogue Card Number 88-91097

ISBN 0-9620546-0-7

BARLOW PRINTING INCORPORATED

409 First Street, Petaluma, CA 94952

This book is dedicated to all the fine officers who served on Alcatraz Island and especially to those who gave their lives on one lovely spring day in May 1946:

Officer William Miller
Officer Harold Stites

Their sons and daughters were my schoolmates.

and

To the memory of my father and mother with whom I was fortunate enough to have spent many wonderful childhood years on Alcatraz Island.

Our Island Home

In Nineteen Hundred and Thirty Four,
   Alcatraz Island opened its door
To a group of men, who were sent
   By the U.S. Federal Government
To guard those men who were doing time
   For committing a terrible Federal crime.

Soon the families of these stalwart men,
   (There were just a few of us then),
Came from towns and cities far away,
   To settle on this Island out in the Bay;
They adjusted themselves without a moan,
   And soon they called this Island their home.

Ere long, more families reached its shore,
   The population grew more and more;
Finally a Post Office, library, grocery store,
   A church, Sunday School opened their door,
Various clubs soon began to form,
   Lo and behold: a little town was born.

Our children were active in many sports,
   Their entertainments were of many sorts,
They rode the Island launch each day,
   To attend city schools across the Bay,
Joys were many, sorrows few,
   As our children to adults grew.

In Nineteen Hundred and Sixty Three,
   The U.S. Goverment did agree
That Alcatraz Island close its door,
   Close down its prison forever more;
So it was that this Island of Fame,
   A lonely Island now became.

To all of those who called it home,
   Who once its many paths did roam,
Who shared its many joys of life,
   Who stood by it in time of strife,
Our Alcatraz home will ever be,
   Not lonely! But cherished in our memory.

Esther Faulk
Reprinted by permission in memory of Lt. Ike Faulk

My brother and I sitting atop an old Army cannon located on the cliff at the South/West end of Alcatraz Island. The cannon along with others was placed there during the Civil War. In 1943 it was removed and used for the scrap effort of World War II. (Picture taken in 1942)

INTRODUCTION

My father was employed for nearly thirty years as a correctional officer with the U.S. Bureau of Prisons. During that time he served over eleven years (1942–1953) on Alcatraz Island. My mother, brother, and I all lived on the island during this period. I was seven years old when my family moved to the island, and eighteen years old when my father retired from the Federal Prison Service in 1953.

After moving from the area over thirty years ago and returning in 1985, I felt the time had arrived to share this wonderful experience I had living a small part of history. I felt that this book was also a very special way I could say thanks to the memory of my father and mother for an exceptional childhood.

The book will take the reader through the history of Alcatraz from the time it was discovered and named to its period as a U.S. Army Fortress; and onto its final phase as America's most famous penitentiary. I believe the book deals in a positive manner with most areas of life on Alcatraz Island when it functioned as a federal prison. This would include the inmates, officers, and their dependents.

Notation: Four names have been changed to protect the privacy of individuals. The four ficticious names are: Gary, Pickett, Joan, and Susan.

CONTENTS

PREFACE

We live in such a fast-paced society that our heritage and history are sometimes lost in the shuffle. This book was undertaken so that all Americans might be able to preserve just a corner of that history for future generations. The book allows everyone not only to know what it was like to grow up on "The Rock", but also to read about the workings of the prison itself. Through pictures of buildings, structures, prison scenes, and more the reader will get a feel for just what made Alcatraz Island so unique among all other prisons.

Alcatraz Island was a federal penitentiary for just under three decades. Why was it established? Why did it close? These are questions that the book will try to answer, along with the question, What was the twenty-nine year "Alcatraz experiment" all about? As to whether or not it was a success must be left up to the experts in the field. The reader can draw his or her own conclusions. Make no mistake about it, though, Alcatraz Island Federal Penitentiary was an experiment from the day it opened in August 1934.

The experiment was, however, more than just an idea pulled out of a hat. Prison authorities were initiating a new concept for dealing with a small but hard core, and possibly violent, population of inmates. The Federal Prison Bureau was forming a policy statement to the entire federal inmate population:

If you try to escape—Alcatraz will take you.

If you can't get along with your fellow inmates—Alcatraz will take you.

But remember, when you come to Alcatraz, we will tell you when to talk, when to eat, what to wear, when to take a shower, and even when to get a haircut. The only decision you will make is when to go to the toilet.

One must remember that an inmate is not in the Federal Prison System by the system's choice. He is there because he chose to disobey federal law. He was

1

transferred to Alcatraz because he had little or no concern for his fellow inmates at another prison. I imagine that long before this man reached "The Rock" he had little respect for himself.

So this was the Federal Prison Bureau's mandate for Alcatraz Island – not to rehabilitate the inmate, but to make him conform, possibly for the first time in his life.

Against this backdrop I spent my childhood years growing up on Alcatraz Island.

Donald J. Hurley ©1987
Alcatraz Island 1942–1953

ONE

History Of Alcatraz Island

After Juan Cabrillo discovered California in 1542, he sailed up the coast, passing by the entrance to the San Francisco Bay without ever seeing it. The same was true of Sir Francis Drake some 35 years later. The missed sightings can probably be attributed to the shroud of fog which covers the harbor entrance almost continuously. It would be another 200 years before the discovery of the San Francisco Harbor, and then it would be by land.

In September of 1769 Gaspar de Portola, who was Military Governor of Upper California, led an expedition north from San Diego for the purpose of finding a land route to Monterey Bay. He sent out two smaller expeditions in a final attempt to find Monterey, which had been discovered by sea in the 16th Century. One of the two expeditions was led by Sergeant Ortega, who took his group north. After some days of heading in this direction, Sergeant Ortega came to a hill that overlooked San Francisco Bay. He knew this was a different bay from the one for which he had been searching. Alcatraz Island, which Ortega observed in the bay, was not named, however, until another Spaniard, Captain Ayala sailed into the harbor in 1775. Captain Ayala, who was commissioned to do a survey of the harbor, noted in his log that the small, rocky island in the bay did not have suitable anchorage or shelter for ships. He did notice that the island had several hundred nesting pelicans on it, so Ayala named it "Isla de Los Alcatraces," which translates to "Island of the Pelicans."

The Spanish and the Mexicans who followed could find little use for the island. It was not until shortly after California became a state in 1850 that the U.S. Army began building a fortress on the island to protect bay area settlers. It took

The first permanent lighthouse on the west coast was completed on Alcatraz Island in 1854 and became operational that same year. Courtesy of Golden Gate National Recreation Area.

several appropriations from Congress to finally get construction on Alcatraz under way.

The man responsible for completing the fortress on Alcatraz was Lieutenant James B. McPherson. Although he disliked his assignment at Alcatraz, he worked tirelessly toward its completion. Finally, in 1859, U.S. Army troops occupied Fort Alcatraz. The name given to the fort by the War Department was officially Post of Alcatraz Island, however, Lieutenant McPherson liked the first name better, and even today some records reflect the title Fort Alcatraz. Whatever name it had, Alcatraz Island became the first permanent fortress on the West Coast.

Lieutenant McPherson, after serving about four years at the Post of Alcatraz Island, was promoted and given a command during the Civil War. By the time he died in battle in 1864, he had attained the rank of Major General.

Plans to build a lighthouse were conceived at the same time the fortress was proposed. The lighthouse was completed in 1854 and in operation the same year. The Alcatraz Lighthouse, like the fortress, became the first on the West Coast. The lighthouse was in operation for fifty-five years before it was replaced in 1909 by a new one, which was gutted by fire in 1970. The tower survived. However, since 1963 the light has been fully automated.

As there has always been a problem with fog on the island, the army discovered early that they needed a means of warning ships when they came too close to shore. In 1857 the army erected a one-half ton fog bell. It sounded when the bell was struck by a heavy metal ball attached to an iron rod. The bell worked on a pulley system. It had to be wound by hand, which took one man about an hour to accomplish. The system was not very effective, but in those days it was the best they had. During the eleven years this writer resided on the island, there were two modern fog horns in place, one at each end of the island. Not one ship ran aground when it was foggy, although there were a couple of near misses.

Early in the development of Alcatraz, it seemed inevitable that the island would become a prison. Within ten years after the army had taken possession of Alcatraz, the fortress was already temporarily housing a few army prisoners from the Presidio for minor offenses. Because the island had been designed as a fortification to protect San Francisco Harbor, lodging prisoners presented a problem. Army personnel had to be shifted from artillery duty to guard the prisoners,

5

This one-half ton fog bell was erected on Alcatraz in 1857 to warn off ships during foggy weather. Courtesy of Golden Gate National Recreation Area.

thus leaving gun posts undermanned. A small wooden structure was built to house the army prisoners, but by the mid 1860's their numbers had grown to well over one hundred, necessitating the construction of a large brick building to house them. All the attempts to resolve the growing prisoner population with proper confinement facilities were no more than band-aid approaches. Records from the 1870's indicate over one hundred and fifty military prisoners in custody serving time, while the army continued to build on a piecemeal basis in order to accommodate them. By the turn of the century, it was apparent that the fortress on Alcatraz was no longer a fort per se, but a full blown military prison. The prison was housing over four hundred military prisoners by now and their crimes consisted of just about everything imaginable. The military prisoner population confined on the island at that time exceeded by one-half times the inmates incarcerated when Alcatraz eventually became a federal penitentiary. It was finally decided by the War Department in 1907 to build a permanent prison. Work on the main structure began soon after and continued until it was completed in 1912. The real irony of this was that the same men who helped build the new prison were also the first to be housed in it.

Post Alcatraz was about to go through its final phase. In 1915 the prison officially became a military disciplinary barracks (an army rehabilitation center for training) and would continue in that capacity for another nineteen years.

During the many years that Alcatraz was a military fortress and then a prison, a number of support buildings were constructed by the army, some of which remained in use until Alcatraz closed as a federal prison in 1963. For example: Old 64 Building, which is a three story structure overlooking the boat dock, was built in 1905 and housed military guards. This writer had an uncle who served as one of these guards during the early 1920's. This building also served as the writer's first home on Alcatraz in 1942. The building is still standing today and can be seen as one disembarks from one of the present day tour boats.

By 1933 the Department of Justice had decided to convert Alcatraz Island into a federal penitentiary. So the U.S. Army prepared to transfer the island to the authority of the Department of Justice, who in turn would place it under their correctional institutional arm, the Bureau of Prisons. No expense was spared in making the prison ready for some of the most notorious inmates in the federal prison system. The entire prison was refurbished. The prison building was completely reinforced. Thick window bars were installed and security doors were replaced. Several gun ports and gun cages were put in place.

The man who became "The Rock's" first warden, James A. Johnston, was to hold that position for fourteen years. He supervised every phase of upgrading the old army prison. Every modern innovation that would help make Alcatraz escape-proof was employed. For instance, full-body metal detectors were installed at key locations to cut down on the movement of contraband. As work progressed on the island, it was clear that some city and county officials around the bay area were very upset to think that an ultra maximum security prison was to be located right in the middle of San Francisco Bay. Warden Johnston gave many detailed tours to these officials in order to alleviate their fear of possible escapes. Finally the day arrived, and on August 11, 1934, Alcatraz Island opened as a federal penitentiary.

SOME OF "THE ROCK'S" MOST INFAMOUS INMATES

Robert "Birdman of Alcatraz" Stroud (AZ#594)

Served 1942-1959, Charge: Murder

Alfonse "Scarface" Capone (AZ#85)

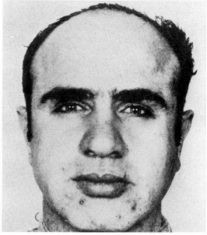

Served 1934-1939, Charge: Tax Violations

Alvin "Creepy" Karpis (AZ#325)

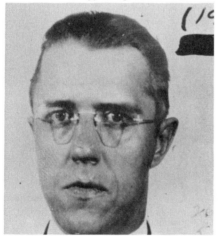

Served 1936-1962, Charge: Kidnapping

George "Machine Gun" Kelly (AZ#117)

Served 1934-1951, Charge: Kidnapping

Inmates at work in one of the many industry work shops. Although inmates began working in these as soon as the prison opened, it was not until 1942 that they received pay for their labor. Courtesy of Golden Gate National Recreation Area.

TWO

The Prison—How It Operated
The Inmate—How He Served His Time

The first inmates to take up residence on Alcatraz were transferred to the island from McNeil Island and Atlanta Federal Prisons. Later they came from other prisons within the system. There were, however, thirty-two U.S. Army Prisoners who were left in Warden Johnston's custody when the army turned over the island to the Department of Justice.

During its first few years as a federal prison, Alcatraz was host to several infamous inmates. The prison opened at the height of the gangster era of the 1930's, and it appeared that the Bureau of Prisons was making every attempt to locate all of the gangsters in one place—Alcatraz.

Possibly the most famous man to serve time on "The Rock" was Al "Scarface" Capone. He served almost five years between 1934 and 1939. As syphillis slowly affected his brain, it was decided by authorities to transfer him to Terminal Island Federal Penitentiary. This is where my father first met him at the prison infirmary. My brother said recently, while I was doing research into famous prisoners on the island, that he remembers my father speaking to our mother one afternoon after talking to Capone. He told her that Capone was showing the signs of his disease and that he had two X's on his chart, which meant that the syphilis was in its second of three stages. Capone was transferred to a prison back East, and within a year he was released to live out the remainder of his life on his estate located in Miami. He died in 1947.

Another famous inmate who served time on Alcatraz, was Robert "Birdman of Alcatraz" Stroud. He actually became somewhat of a celebrity for his care and feeding of birds while at Leavenworth Federal Prison. One can still purchase his

Visitation rights on "The Rock" consisted of talking into a two way phone and looking at each other through five inches of bullet proof glass. Courtesy of Golden Gate National Recreation Area.

books on the subject. A movie was made of his life in 1962 in order to put pressure on the Department of Justice to gain his freedom. It was to no avail, however, as Stroud died in 1963 at the federal medical facility in Springfield, Missouri. He was transferred there from Alcatraz in 1959 as his health began to deteriorate. Prison officials felt that to release Stroud would be a mistake even though he had served over fifty years in prisons. Seventeen of those years were served on Alcatraz. The decision not to release him was based on the nature of his crimes. He had killed twice, once while in prison. He killed a man in Alaska in an argument concerning a dance hall girl (Alaska was a Federal Territory at the time). Then, while serving time for the first murder, he stabbed an officer to death in the dining room at Leavenworth Prison in 1916. Stroud arrived on Alcatraz about the same time my family moved onto the island.

One day while I was talking to my father several years after he retired, I asked him of all the famous inmates who served time on the island, which one caused the least trouble? Without a moment's hesitation, he answered that it would have to be George "Machine Gun" Kelly. My father said that from the time Kelly arrived on Alcatraz in 1934 until he was transferred in 1951 due to a heart condition, he served his time without incident. He died of a heart attack in 1954 in the Federal Prison at Leavenworth.

The list of famous criminals who have served time on Alcatraz Island goes on and on. There was "Doc" Barker of the Ma Barker Gang and Alvin Karpis who was number one on the F.B.I.'s most wanted list during the early 1930's.

At first, prison bureau officials made no pretense about rehabilitating inmates on Alcatraz. They were there to serve time and nothing more. Good time served and extra yard privileges for working in one of the shops, etc. were about the only things an inmate had to look forward to. After the gangster era ended in the late 1930's, prisoners were transferred to "The Rock" for a new set of reasons, such as causing problems at other federal prisons.

Warden Johnston knew that just housing inmates could become a real problem. Whenever men had an excessive amount of time on their hands, their thoughts would turn to other things, which included the ever-present danger of escape. The warden knew that men who were serving long sentences, as most of the inmates on "The Rock" were, had to have some outlet for their pent up

A view of the six "dark" or "hole" cells in (D) Block.

emotions. Suicide, surprisingly enough, never became a real problem among the inmates. Alcatraz had a much lower suicide rate than most other prisons within the system.

Warden Johnston was well aware of the fact that as the 30's came to a close the type of prisoner arriving on the island was changing. Instead of the gangster type criminal, he was now the lone bank robber or murderer, etc.... Most of these inmates had been troublemakers at other prisons. The warden implemented a work/reward program as soon as possible. Prior to World War II there were not many jobs for the inmates, but with less than 280 prisoners, he knew it could work. However, it was not until 1942 that pay for work became a reality.

The inmates had to earn their jobs with good behavior time. Then they were allowed to work in such shops as furniture, mat, laundry, and others. Money and good time were the warden's incentives. Keep in mind, though, that Alcatraz still had as its primary purpose to control the inmate and make him conform.

During the first years of the prison's operation inmates were not allowed to talk to each other or to have more than one visit per month from a blood relative or wife. No visits were allowed to inmates the first three months after their arrival. When a visit was requested, the visitor had to apply in writing to the warden. When approved, the warden would send a letter back to the party advising them to be on the dock at Pier 4 in San Francisco with the letter to show the boat officer. Once on the island, the visitor would be transported by vehicle up to the prison. He or she would then walk through a full-body metal detector. The visit was conducted through one of five visitor stations by talking into phones and looking at each other through five inches of bullet-proof glass. Some policies were relaxed, such as the "rule of silence" in 1937. Inmates could also correspond with more than one relative by 1940.

There was a complete head count of the inmates several times a day. An inmate could not bank on routine counts however, especially when locked up, as a surprise inspection of his cell could occur at any time day or night. Head counts of the cells later averaged every hour. Most inmates spent an average of thirteen hours each day locked in their cells.

The prison itself was made up of four cell blocks. There was (A) Block which was used during the military occupation but not utilized by prison authorities.

A typical five feet wide by nine feet long cell. Courtesy of Golden Gate National Recreation Area.

It was referred to as the Army Block. (B) and (C) Blocks consisted of cells three tiers high. (D) Block consisted of several solitary confinement cells where inmates were kept in "lock-up" all the time or until they were allowed to join the rest of the prison population. There were also six dark cells or the hole, called "Hot Box" by the inmates. I will comment more about these cells in a minute.

Each regular cell was approximately five feet wide by nine feet long. Each contained a bunk, wash basin, toilet, and a shelf to hold various items. There was also an uncovered light bulb located in the center of the cell and positioned directly overhead. One man to a cell was the policy of the authorities for the entire twenty-nine year history of "The Rock" as a federal prison. The dark or hole cells were somewhat larger than the other cells; however, they contained nothing. There was no bunk, toilet, or wash basin. There were four walls and a floor with a drain in the center. Each one of the six cells had an overhead light, but they were controlled from outside the cells. At one time all the cells except one contained toilets, etc., but due to damage caused by the inmates, all these items were removed. The cells each had two metal doors, and when an inmate was locked in, he was in total darkness and silence. The hole was used as a disciplinary tool when inmates would blatantly violate prison rules. Inmates were kept in these cells indefinitely, depending on the severity of the offense.

The prison yard was located at the northwest end of the prison. It was enclosed by high concrete walls with a fence extending another six feet above that. The yard afforded inmates an opportunity to exercise and get a little fresh air. Although there were large numbers of inmates in the dining area, talking was kept to a minimum. This was not the case in the prison yard, where prisoners were allowed to talk and mix. The most popular game in the yard was hand ball. There were two courts, a large one for the good players and a small one for the novice. Once in a while some of the inmates would get a baseball game going. I remember they used a little ball that the island kids called a hard-soft ball. It was somewhat larger than a hardball, but much smaller than a softball. The ball had a very hard cover. Once in awhile an inmate would hit a ball over the wall, and an officer on his way home from "up top" (the prison area) might find it and give it to one of the kids.

Time in the prison yard was not the only period during the day that inmates

Inmates engaged in a game of baseball in the prison yard. When inmates climbed the bleacher type stairs at the right to enter the prison they could look out over the wall and see San Francisco less than a mile and a half away. Courtesy of Golden Gate National Recreation Area.

were away from their cells. Other than prisoners who were confined to their cells in (D) Block (solitary confinement) all the time, or an occasional inmate locked up in the "hole" for some type of disciplinary action, most were out working. There were several work details to which the inmates were assigned, such as the various industry buildings, kitchen and dining areas, cell house area itself, and around the dock area. There were also certain details scheduled during the week. There was the garbage detail, laundry delivery detail, and several clean-up details. The last three involved inmates working around the officer's dependents and housing.

During World War II the newly completed laundry building became the most active work area on the island. Laundry was done for the Army Presidio, Fort Mason, Angel Island and, of course, all the prison. Inmates also worked on Navy nets and buoys, some of which were used in the massive submarine net under the Golden Gate Bridge. The dock was a very busy place during the war as all the laundry was loaded and unloaded there by the officers and army people. This involved the assignment of several more officers to the area, as inmates were not allowed on board ships. They moved goods once cargo was unloaded.

No matter how busy Alcatraz Island's inmates became, the prison routine never varied. It was very rigid and inmates had to conform to a very strict time table. Without going into great detail, here is a sample of the working inmate's schedule.

6:30 am	Morning gong to get up.
6:50 am	Get ready to leave cell for breakfast.
6:55 am	March single file to mess hall.
7:00 am	Breakfast
7:20 am	Breakfast ends and shop working inmates proceed to rear door that leads to the recreation yard. Inside workers proceed to their inside details and stand-by. (During all the inmates' movements several officers are in place to see that all moved smoothly.)
7:25 am	Shop assigned inmates proceed to their assigned shop details.
7:30 am	All inmates are counted before beginning work.
11:30 am	At 12:00 pm inmates had noon meal and were locked in their cells for a head count.

Inmates returning to the prison from the industrial shop areas. Notice how they must walk through the metal detectors before they climb the stairs, go through the steel door located in the prison yard wall. They then cross the yard and enter the cell house in an open area adjacent to the cell blocks called "Times Square." Courtesy of Golden Gate National Recreation Area.

12:20 pm	Work proceeds same as before.
12:30 pm	Work details counted before beginning assignments.
4:25 pm	All prisoners return to prison building by way of full body metal detectors, then proceed to the mess hall for dinner.
4:50 pm	Return to cells for final lock-up of the day where a stand-up head count is made.

From this point on, cell counts continued till the next morning when the procedure started all over again. Lights were turned off at 9:30 pm.

There were always special details to be taken care of from time to time, such as repairs around the island, filling chuck holes in the road or various painting needs, etc. Prison authorities learned early on that inmates were a source of cheap labor, and it should be noted that many of them possessed highly usable skills.

There was a library from the time the island became a federal prison, and as the years went by, it added volumes, until by 1960 it had a total of 15,000 books. Inmates were allowed to have a total of three library books in their cells, plus a Bible, dictionary, and several study books. Failure to return books to the library on their due date could result in the loss of one's library privileges.

For many of the prisoners though, life must have been just one, dull, routine day after another. The one bright spot for the inmates occurred at meal time. Very few complaints were ever registered about the food on Alcatraz. As a correctional officer, my father was occasionally assigned to either the kitchen or dining area, and would sometimes eat the prison meals. He told me more than once that Alcatraz had the best food of all the federal prisons within the system. As most riots begin in the dining area of any prison, Warden Johnston, while refurbishing the institution, had installed tear gas canisters in the ceiling. If it ever reached the point where officials were unable to maintain control, an officer who was in a special protected area adjacent to the dining room could release the canisters automatically. The canisters were in plain view of the inmates, and I am very sure they had a strong psychological effect on them. The short eating sessions for each meal were also a deterrent to riots. Twenty minutes kept planning to a minimum.

Prisoners were shown movies once a week. Prison officials saw to it that movies were not of a controversial nature—mostly westerns or musicals were shown.

While inmates have a meal in the dining room a small prison combo plays music. Note the canister of tear gas attached to the beam. (upper left area of picture) Courtesy of Golden Gate National Recreation Area.

Movies did not start on the island for the inmates until several years after the prison was open. Movies were shown in the prison chapel, and the inmates looked forward to them each week.

By the 1950's many things changed on Alcatraz. Radio jacks with ear phones were installed in cells. Also, a prison band was formed which played at special events like Thanksgiving or Christmas meals. The inmates were allowed to practice on weekends in the chapel.

Out of all the inmates who served time on Alcatraz, 97½ percent did so without ever trying to escape. In the next chapter we will look at the 2½ percent who did make their bid for freedom. We will see just what fate held in store for them.

Sign located at the south/east end of the island warning of prosecution for anyone who procures or conceals the escape of any prisoners. Courtesy of San Francisco Public Library.

THREE

Escape From Alcatraz—An Inmate's Dream

There were fourteen escape attempts from "The Rock" during its 29 year history as a federal prison. Many felt that more inmates would have tried to escape but for two reasons. First, the temperature in the San Francisco Bay usually hovers around fifty degrees. Second, inmates had reservations about the swift current, which on some days would run at several miles per hour. Just a word about the water current that surrounds the island. On several occasions people have swum around the island, being careful not to get within two hundred yards of the shore. The reason for this was that the undertow and current adjacent to the island was so swift, due to Alcatraz's position in the center of the channel directly in front of the Golden Gate Bridge.

I will relate a personal experience I had regarding the current around the island. I was about fourteen years old. A friend and I were on the beach fishing. The wind was blowing hard and the bay was very rough. My friend was on the beach, while I was standing on a jetty that protruded approximately fifteen feet out into the bay. I slipped and fell into the water. I was in about waist deep and was being pulled along at a very fast pace. It was like running to keep from falling. I let go of my fishing pole and looked towards the beach. My friend stuck out his pole and I grabbed it. He pulled me to the shore, probably saving my life. From that day on I maintained a healthy respect for the current that flowed around the island. I was very fortunate to have lost only my fishing gear.

Following is a history of the escape attempts from Alcatraz Island during its 29 year history. As I stated there were a total of fourteen attempts, involving some 36 inmates. The results were:

Shot and killed	6
Shot and wounded	2
Drowned – confirmed	2
Drowned ? – presumed dead	5
Executed in gas chamber	2
Recaptured – not wounded	19

Almost 30 percent of the inmates who attempted to escape either died in their bid for freedom or later paid with their lives in the gas chamber.

(A note of interest to the reader: After the bloody riot of 1946, which will be covered in the next chapter, there were no attempted escapes from "The Rock" for 10 years.)

April 27, 1936—Joseph Bowers was allowed to work at the island's incinerator, which was located at a lower level ledge overlooking the water on the west side of the island. This area was completely surrounded by a wire fence and was within the view of the officer working in the road tower. About 11:00 am Bowers began climbing the fence in order to drop into the water below. The officer in the tower fired one warning shot, but the inmate continued to climb over the fence, and started down the other side. The officer fired again. This time Bowers was struck by the bullet and, being fatally wounded, fell to the water below. His body was recovered.

December 16, 1937—Ralph Roe and Theodore Coe worked in the mat shop at the north end of the island. An officer checked them at 1:00 pm, but when he returned a while later, neither man was anywhere in sight. The officer observed that the wire mesh to a window had been cut out and a large hole had been made in the window. This window is situated directly over the water. Immediately the alarm was sounded, and boats began to circle the island. Because the fog was so dense that day, the two inmates were never found. Both were believed to have drowned, but to this day they are recorded as officially missing.

April 23, 1938—Rufus Franklin, James Lucas and Thomas Limmerick were working in the furniture factory. They armed themselves with metal scraps and a couple of hammers. When officer Royal C. Cline, who was assigned to that area, entered the room, the inmates jumped him and struck him on the head with a hammer, rendering him unconscious. The inmates then broke out a window and climbed to the top of the building. They encountered some barbed wire which seals off a catwalk that runs around the roof of the building.

There is a tower that sits flush on top of the building roof and on this day it was manned by officer Harold Stites (later killed in the prison riot of 1946). The inmates cut the barbed wire and got onto the catwalk which led to the tower. The three of them crept along the walk until they were at a point where the catwalk runs around the tower. They split up just as the officer saw them. They attacked the tower glass with the hammers. The glass is not bullet proof, but it is shatter proof. Officer Stites pulled his .45 cal. automatic and fired through the glass, striking Limmerick in the head. Inmate Franklin attacked with one of the hammers. Officer Stites fired and struck him in the arm. As the .45 cal. was now empty, Stites unslung his rifle from his shoulder. Just as the wounded Franklin was going to throw his hammer, Officer Stites fired the rifle, striking Franklin in the leg. This ended the assault. By now other officers were arriving to take charge of the scene. Officer Cline and Inmate Limmerick both died as a result of their injuries. Lucas and Franklin (who recovered from his wounds) were given additional life sentences.

January 13, 1939—Arthur "Doc" Barker, Rufus McCain, Dale Stamphill, Henri Young, and William Martin were all in special lock-up in the old army isolation cells in (D) Block, which were in bad shape and should have been replaced years before. All five cut their way through the bars, emerged into the corridor, and cut through a ground floor window. They quickly scambled down the cliff to the beach, but were missed minutes later at the 3:45 am count. The alarm was activated, and the prison launch and coast guard boats responded. All five were captured, but Stamphill and "Doc" Barker tried to jump into the water to escape. Barker struck his head on a rock as he dove into the water. In a hail of bullets Barker was shot several times, while Stamphill received a leg wound. Both were taken to the prison hospital where "Doc" Barker, son of the infamous "Ma" Barker, died the next day of his wounds. Stamphill recovered, and all were given additional time for the attempt.

Twenty-three months later Young, who was in on the ill-fated attempt with Martin and the others, stabbed Martin to death. No reason was ever given for

Officer Stites was on duty in the above industry tower on April 23, 1938 when he was attacked by three escapees with hammers. Officer Stites managed to shoot and kill one and wound another before help arrived. Officer Stites later was killed in the '46 riot. Courtesy of Golden Gate National Recreation Area.

the incident except the rumor that there was bad blood between them over the escape.

May 21, 1941—Joseph Cretzer, Sam Shockley, Lloyd Barkdoll, and Arnold Kyle were assigned to the mat shop. They took three hostages while trying to cut their way through some window bars. The captain, who was making his morning rounds, walked into the shop and was taken hostage also. The captain talked them out of the escape, and the inmates decided to give up. No one was injured. Joseph Cretzer was later killed in the Riot of 1946. Sam Shockley was put to death in the San Quentin gas chamber for his part in the 1946 Riot.

September 15, 1941—John Bayless was assigned to the garbage detail. At the end of the work day, he, along with others who worked at special details, including the dock, were brought to the side of the prison to be counted. That afternoon the fog was thicker than usual. While standing by the prison entrance, the fog suddenly became so thick one inmate could not see the man standing next to him. Bayless took this opportunity to make a dash for it. He ran across a road and down the gradual cliff to the water. Unfortunately for Bayless, several officers were right on his heels and captured him at once.

It should be pointed out that attempted escapes that occur on the spur of the moment would normally fail in any prison. In this type of escape the inmate is either recaptured at once or gets himself killed, as in the first escape.

April 13, 1943—Fred Hunter, Floyd Hamilton, Harold Best and James Boarman were working in the mat shop. They overpowered the duty officer and tied him up. The captain just happened by and was also taken hostage and tied up. The four inmates were able to cut through some wire mesh on a window and make their bid for freedom. This was the first escape attempt from Alcatraz in which my father participated in the recapture of the inmates. He told me some time later, after talking to other officers, that this was the first escape attempt that inmates planned for the cold bay waters by greasing themselves down with machine oil. He also told me that at least two of the inmates, Boarman and Best, had stolen army uniforms from the laundry to wear when they reached the main land. (earlier I told of doing the laundry for the army during World War II)

One of the hostage officers managed to get free and blow his whistle. On that day my father's friend, Frank Johnson, was working in the west tower on top of one of the industrial buildings. He heard the officer's whistle and put in a call for help. He then turned his attention to the waters off the island's west beach. He saw two figures swimming in a westerly direction. He fired several shots at them. The prison launch had just rounded the end of the island and proceeded to cut off the two. As the launch came alongside, the officers on the boat noted that Best was holding up Boarman who had been shot in the head. Best let go of Boarman to board the launch, and at once Boarman slipped below the surface. His body was never recovered. Hunter was found hiding in the rear of a large cave located at the northwest end of the island. The search for Hamilton lasted for another three days. He was discovered hiding in the same building from which he had escaped. He told officers that after spending two days and nights in a cave with the cold tide waters rising and falling, he (Hamilton) decided to return to the mat shop rather than wait to be discovered and probably shot.

Just a note to let the reader know that this writer, after having researched all of the escape attempts from Alcatraz, is of the opinion that with its dismal rate of success the escape attempts must have had a profound impact psychologically on other inmates. After all, there was no guarantee for any inmate who reached the water. As we have seen, he was just as likely to die in the water as he was before he reached it. Records show that of the eight confirmed deaths during escape attempts two were shot in the water and two were confirmed drowned. This does not include the five inmates presumed dead by drowning.

August 7, 1943 – Ted Walters was assigned to work in the laundry. The shop was extremely busy during the war. When Walters thought no one was watching, he left the laundry area and climbed over a fence and started down a cliff towards the water. Unknown to Walters, however, the shop supervisor had missed him almost at once and called in to report a possible escape attempt. By the time Walters was about to enter the water, officers, who had arrived on the cliff above him, ordered Walters to halt. He did, and was taken into custody at once.

July 31, 1945 – John Giles was one of the inmates assigned to the dock area as a gardener and sweeper, doing general clean-up work. He had decided some time earlier to steal an army uniform from the laundry which was always stacked in bundles on the dock. Twice a week the laundry was dropped off and picked up by the steam ship, *General Frank M. Coxe*. Giles saw his opportunity one afternoon. He stole a uniform and slipped behind a building to put it on under his prison clothes. When the *Coxe* had docked, just after 10:00 am, the dock officer had made his count of the dock inmates and then turned away to do something else. Giles took one final glance at the dock tower officer. He was not looking his way so Giles slipped under the pier and stripped off his prison clothes. He then stepped onto the lower rear deck of the *Coxe*.

Just after the *Coxe* pulled away from the dock a head count of the inmates revealed that Giles was missing. As the *Coxe* was too far away from the island, the dock officer immediately called the associate warden's office and advised him Giles was missing. The dock officer said that he thought Giles might have boarded the *Coxe*, which was enroute to Angel Island, a distance of about five miles. The associate warden called the military police at Angel Island. Then he summoned a couple of officers and raced down to the dock, boarded one of the island's boats, and proceeded to Angel Island. Giles was picked up within a couple of minutes after the *Coxe* had docked at Angel Island. He was returned to Alcatraz on the *Coxe's* next run—handcuffed and in the company of the officers. He received the customary five year addition to his sentence for his attempt at a bid for freedom.

I remember this incident very well. A friend and I were walking along the lower balcony of the residence building that overlooked the dock. We noticed that several officers were searching the dock area, but we did not know exactly what they were looking for. A few minutes later, the *Coxe* docked and off stepped this guy in an army uniform, handcuffed and between two officers. Seeing this, it did not take my friend or me very long to figure out just what had happened.

May 2, 1946—(Known as the Alcatraz Riot) We will address this attempted escape in the next chapter.

July 26, 1956—Floyd P. Wilson was also assigned to the dock. After one of several head counts during the day, Wilson disappeared. He managed to hide from searching officers for over eleven hours by concealing himself between two buildings. He was planning to wait until dark and then float to his freedom on a large ball of wrapping cord, which was used to tie up laundry bundles. He was eventually located and placed in solitary confinement.

September 20, 1958—Aaron Burgett and Clyde Johnson were working on

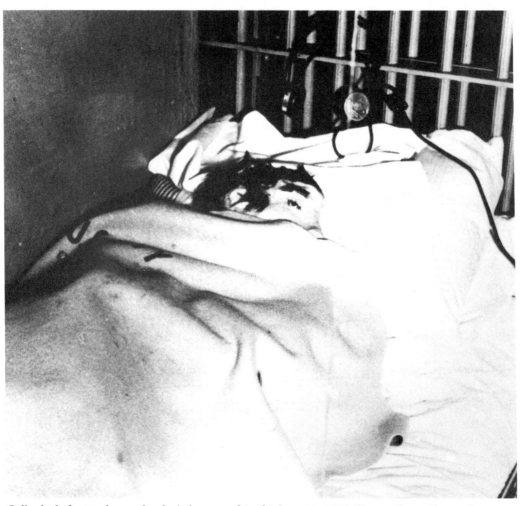

Cell which depicts dummy head of plaster used in the June 11, 1962 "Escape From Alcatraz" attempt. Courtesy of Golden Gate National Recreation Area.

the garbage detail when they overpowered an officer and raced toward the water. This was not a spur-of-the-moment escape attempt, as both inmates had made crude snorkels, face masks, etc. After they entered the water, the men got separated and Johnson was captured within an hour. Burgett, however, was not so lucky. He drowned, and his body was not recovered for nearly two weeks.

June 11, 1962 – (Known as "Escape from Alcatraz") An escape attempt was made by three inmates. They were Frank Morris, John Anglin and his brother Clarence Anglin. The planning for this escape was the most elaborate in the prison's history. The inmates appropriated hair from the prison barber shop and glued it onto plaster dummy heads which they had made. They also stole at least three raincoats and fastened them together so they could be used as a life raft. All the materials taken were kept on top of the cell block just under the prison roof. With the dummy heads in their bunks, the three inmates, who had chipped out the rear vents of their cells, could climb up to the top of the cell tier unnoticed. There they could work on cutting the overhead fan vent bars, which led to the prison's roof. Months after the planning had begun everything was finally ready to go. The three men waited until after the 9:35 pm cell count before leaving. This would give them a nine hour head start, as bed checks at night were only visual, made by officers from outside the cells. Before the inmates squeezed out through the vents at the rear of their cells, they put the dummy heads in their bunks to make them appear as if they were occupied. After the three had squeezed through the vents in the cells and pulled the vents back into place behind themselves, they proceeded to climb to the top of the cell block tier. Now they had to remove the part of the overhead vent which had been cut. Once it was removed, the three of them squeezed through the vent and onto the prison roof. The last inmate passed up the rubber raincoats and rope which they would need to lower themselves down the prison wall. After lowering themselves to the ground, the three inmates next climbed over a fence and made their way to the water. They have never been seen since.

Many theories have been advanced regarding their complete disappearance. Some believe that they had a boat pick them up. After all, they had over nine hours without anyone looking for them. Another theory is that because they had

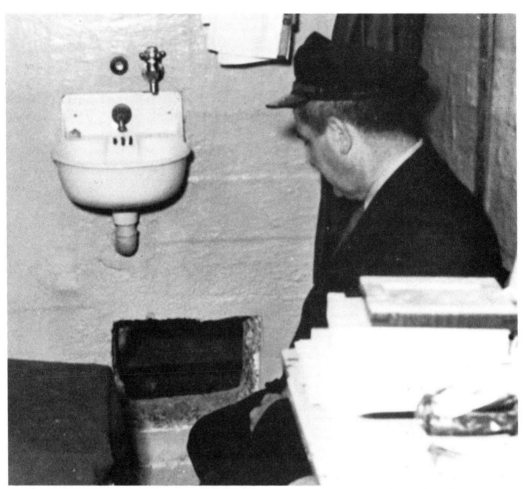

Officer views one of three cells which depicts a hole cut out at rear of cell which allowed Morris, and the Anglin brothers to escape the prison building. Courtesy of Golden Gate National Recreation Area.

some location, made it to either Angel Island or San Francisco. The third possibility is that they drowned.

A duffle bag was recovered, washed up on a beach in the northern part of the bay in Marin County. This occurred several days after the escape attempt. The bag contained a money order in Clarence Anglin's name. At this point the search was intensified but nothing else ever turned up.

December 16-1962 - Lee Parker and John P. Scott made their bid for freedom by prying open a window of a storeroom located below the prison kitchen. They climbed to the roof of the prison, crossed over to the other side, and lowered themselves down the side of the building. They were lucky that no one had observed them, as it was broad daylight. They proceeded down to the water at the northwest end of the island. As soon as they were missed, a massive search was conducted on the island and on the water. Several coast guard boats as well as both prison launches were involved. Parker was captured clinging to some rocks just off the northwest end of the island known as "Little Alcatraz". Scott was found several miles from Alcatraz near Fort Point by the Golden Gate Bridge. He had made it that far with the help of simple inflatable gloves. He was found more dead than alive, however, he did recover.

It is interesting to note that all but three of the attempts to escape took place in late spring, summer or fall. This would indicate that potential escapees must have given some thought to the weather. During its 29 year history as a prison, an average of one escape every two years was attempted. The real exception to this was that after the bloody riot of 1946, there were no attempts at escape for over ten years.

Many people have made the statement over the years that Alcatraz Island was our country's answer to France's Devil's Island. Allow me to make a few comparisons. Although both are islands, Devil's Island is several miles off the coast of the northeast tip of South America, while Alcatraz is in the middle of San Francisco Bay, less than one and one half miles from shore. The weather on Alcatraz is usually fair during the daylight hours, becoming foggy, windy and damp most every evening. Devil's Island is in a tropical area with very hot and humid weather. There were many life threatening problems for Devil's Island inhabitants. Both prisoners and guards alike had to worry about such things as venomous snakes, various fevers, and quicksand swamps. Capital offenses could be dealt with right on the spot by the prison superintendent on Devil's Island. An escape attempt could result in six months in solitary confinement and several years added to a sentence. A second offense of attempted escape could, at the superintendent's discretion, result in death by the guillotine. There was no trial or any form of due process of law. Many of the prisoners were sent to Devil's Island for political reasons. This was never the case at Alcatraz. So, it would appear that even with a quick comparison of the two, they were as different as day and night. Devil's Island was closed in 1951, while Alcatraz functioned as a federal prison until 1963.

Just about everyone believed that Alcatraz Island was closed as a prison due in part to the June 11, 1962 escape. It did, in fact, draw attention to the deterioration not only of the main prison building, but also to the cost of refurbishing several structures on the island. It was estimated that in 1963 it would cost nearly six million dollars just to bring the main prison building up to an acceptable standard. Just about all the buildings, especially the metal structures (towers, etc.), had taken a beating over the years from the weather. The wind, fog, and salt air were, however, just some of the reasons that Alcatraz was shut down.

There were seldom more than 280 inmates on the island at any one time, add to that a correctional officers' force of almost 90 (which, by the way, was the highest ratio rate of officers to inmates of any federal prison in the system: 1 to 3.1.). The Justice Department also noted that to keep an inmate on Alcatraz cost $13.80 per day. The average for all other prisons in the federal system was nearly one third of that or approximately $5.40.

Therefore, it was decided by Attorney General Robert F. Kennedy that Alcatraz Island would be closed as a federal penitentiary no later than June 30, 1963, because the operation of the prison was not cost effective. The officers and inmates were to be transferred to other federal institutions.

The lighthouse, which had been under the watchful eye of man for one hundred and nine years, fell victim to modern technology by being placed on full automation.

One of the officers retired and remained after the island had been turned over to the U.S. General Service Department to ensure the island's integrity against trespassing.

So, on March 21, 1963, the twenty-nine year experiment came to an end. I am sure that if Warden Johnston could have been there that day, he surely would have remarked disappointedly that America's legendary prison was passing into history.

Some of Alcatraz Island's children, unable to return home due to prison riot. Photograph taken on Pier 4 in San Francisco. The boy standing next to the girl and looking directly at the camera is the writer. (Picture taken May 2, 1946) Courtesy of AP/Wide World Photos

FOUR

Alcatraz Riot—1946

May 2, 1946, was the first of two of the bloodiest days in the history of Alcatraz. I will remember this tragic event as long as I live. My first recollection of that day was walking down Pier 4 in San Francisco on a lovely spring day. Several children and myself were on our way from school to catch the 3:35 pm boat home to the island. About half way down the pier, we heard the escape siren begin wailing from across the water. Everyone on the pier just looked at each other knowing full well what it meant. There was a prison break in progress.

The prison launch never showed up for its 3:35 pm scheduled run. Two of the officers' wives were on the dock and told us that their husbands had returned to the island a few minutes before on a coast guard boat. Some of the swing shift and off-duty officers began arriving on the dock. My father was among this group. I told my father what the two officers' wives had related to us earlier. A few minutes later the Army Steamship *Frank M. Coxe* arrived from Angel Island, but refused to transport any of the waiting officers to Alcatraz. More children and working mothers began arriving on the dock. This group included my mother who had taken a job as a civilian worker at Fort Mason, which is located adjacent to Pier 4.

Finally the prison launch, which had been patrolling off the island, was seen heading around the end of the island towards the dock. Thirty minutes later it rounded the island and headed in our direction. It was nearly 7:00 pm by the time it arrived at Pier 4. When the boat had tied up, one officer was carried off completely covered with a blanket. He was placed in an ambulance, which left the dock area immediately. The evening and off-duty officers boarded the launch

39

and headed off into the night. No one had any idea where the women and children were going to stay that evening. As it turned out we spent two nights at the Stewart Hotel in San Francisco.[1] We returned to our homes on the island Saturday, May 4, 1946.

Over the next several weeks almost every conversation was about the riot. I had talked to several of the children, whose fathers had told them the parts they had played in this bloody riot. My father had very little to say about the riot until several years later. He then related his experience of the event to me. I also have had a chance to talk to several of the officers who worked on the island at the time of the riot.

Every year I see some of them at our annual get together of the "Alcatraz Alumni Association." Over the years I have been able to put together a fairly accurate account of what actually took place.

It appears that there were six ring leaders in the botched escape attempt. They were Joseph Cretzer, Bernie Coy, Marvin Hubbard, Myron Thompson, Sam Shockley (known as "Crazy Sam") and Clarence Carnes. Among them, the six inmates were serving a total of 274 years plus three life terms. Inmate Coy had fashioned some type of metal spreaders out of machine shop scraps and hid them in the bottom of his cell toilet. He left them there until it was time for the breakout.

Coy's work detail was mopping and general cleanup in the cell house area. On the day of the escape attempt, Coy was mopping the prison floor between (B) and (C) Blocks. He was joined by Hubbard who had arrived from his detail in the kitchen. The two inmates then overpowered officer Miller who was on duty in the cell block area. They dragged Miller down the cell block and dumped him in Cell 403, which was open and empty as was the adjacent Cell 402. Coy then went to the cell officers desk and removed the cell block keys. These keys unlocked the safety covers that controlled the manual opening and closing of the cells. Inmate Coy next got his spreaders and climbed up to the bars surrounding the West Gun Gallery, which overlooked all the cell blocks. He placed the make-shift spreaders between the horizontal gallery bars. Then, after a little work, he man-

---

[1] Courtesy of the Red Cross

Officer inspects area of west gun gallery where Inmate Coy climbed up, spread the bars and over powered an officer in the bloodiest riot in the prison's history. Courtesy of Golden Gate National Recreation Area.

aged to spread the bars to the gallery wide enough to allow him to squeeze through. He then waited for gallery officer Burch to return from (D) Block. Within a few minutes Burch unlocked the door and stepped inside. (The gun gallery's entrance is from outside the cell block, but still within the prison.) The inmate immediately accosted the officer, and after a prolonged struggle, Coy gained the upper hand. He got hold of Burch's rifle, struck him in the head rendering him unconscious. He then took the officer's rifle and removed his holster retrieving the only other weapon in the gallery, which was a .45 caliber automatic. He also took several rounds of ammunition for both weapons as well as billy clubs, and all the keys he could lay his hands on.

The one thing inmate Coy did not know at the time was that the only key which would allow him and his fellow conspirators to leave the interior of the prison was not in the West Gun Gallery. The key (#107) was in the possession of officer Miller who had failed to return it to the gallery after an early lunch. Coy handed down his booty to other inmates who were by now gathered in Cell Block (D). The prisoner's plan was to get weapons, take as many hostages as possible, unlock the yard door in order to get outside the prison. The ultimate target—the boat.

As time progressed, other officers entered the cell house area looking for men who had failed to report in. They too were overpowered and taken to Cells 402 and 403. Eventually the inmates had taken a total of eight officers hostage.

The inmates had realized sometime before that key #107 was missing. This key would have given them access to the door, which led to the prison yard. The prisoners suspected that Officer Miller had the key, so Cretzer went to Cell 403 and had Miller brought out and beaten. However, unknown to the inmates, Officer Miller had put the key down the toilet of Cell 403 prior to being searched and beaten. The six ring leaders were well aware of the fact that without key #107 any thought of escape was hopeless.

Frustrated and angry, Coy took the rifle to a cell house window located on the east side of the building. From that point he had a view of the officer in the dock tower. He took a shot at him, but fortunately missed. He then went to the dining area of the building where he had a good view of the officer in the hill tower. Coy shot at him, striking the officer in the leg. Coy jumped up and

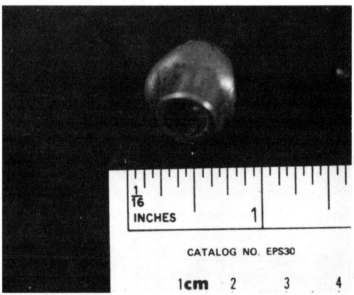

Two .45 caliber slugs fired from inside the prison at officers outside. The above two just missed my father and he managed to recover them. (Prison riot 1946)

down yelling "I got one of them!" Coy then decided to check the cell one more time for the key. He went into the cell where officer Miller and several other officers, were being held. Coy searched all the officers again. He finally checked the toilet and found the key.

Coy ran out of the cell and told the other inmates that he had found the key. He went at once to the door that led to the prison yard and tried the key. He discovered that another key was jammed in the lock. After working on it for sometime, he forced out the jammed key, but to his dismay, he found that the lock was so chewed up that key #107 would not unlock the door. The inmates knew at this point that it was all but over.

At this time "Crazy Sam" Shockley told Cretzer, who had the .45 caliber automatic, to "kill all of the S.O.B.'s" in the cells. Cretzer obliged and fired several rounds point blank into both the hostage cells, wounding five officers.

Cretzer then took the .45 caliber and went to one of the windows in (D) Block and fired through it at several officers who were just outside the building. Two of the bullets almost struck my father. He managed to retrieve the two slugs.

Just after midnight on Friday (May 3), Lt.'s Ike Faulk and Fred Roberts entered the cell house in search of the hostage officers. Each had a team of five volunteers. As the lights had been turned off in the cell house, the two teams had to move very cautiously. They knew that at least two of the inmates were armed, however, Warden Johnston would not allow the officers to take weapons into the cell house. Once inside the two teams split up.[2] Lt. Roberts and his team were checking cell blocks (B) and (C) on Broadway when inmate Cretzer fired down upon them from on top of the (C) Block tier, striking Lt. Roberts twice. Lt. Faulk had better luck. He was checking on the other side of (C) Block (Seedy Street). His team discovered the hostages about the same time Cretzer was firing down at Lt. Roberts' team. As soon as the shooting started Lt. Phil Bergen and his team, who had been in the West Gun Gallery for sometime and had earlier rescued Officer Burch, began spraying the top of (C) Block tier with machine gun fire allowing Roberts' team to get him (Roberts) out of the area. Lt. Faulk removed all the hostages to safety.

---

[2] Refer to sketch on page 45.

Utility corridor where three inmates died. Refer to #12 below sketch. Courtesy of Golden Gate National Recreation Area.

1 – Main Cellhouse
2 – Prison Yard
3 – Kitchen
4 – Dining Room
5 – Six Dark Cells
6 – Library
7 – Administration
8 – Warden's Office
9 – West Road Tower
10 – West Gun Gallery
11 – East Gun Gallery
12 – Utility Corridor where
    three inmates were killed
13 – Hospital above
14 – Door that leads to
    Prison Yard from Cellhouse
15 – Stairs to (A) Block

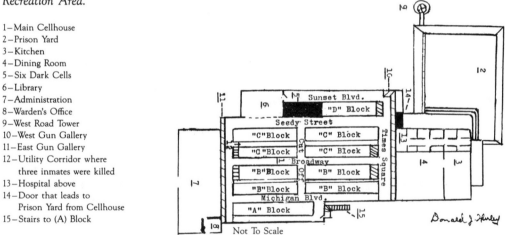

Sketch of cell house, dining room, kitchen, hospital, prison yard and road tower.

Later Friday night (May 3), the Marines began dropping concussion grenades through holes which they drilled in the roof for that purpose. Three of the ring leaders returned to their cells, hoping no one would find out they were involved. Officials determined that Cretzer, Coy, and Hubbard had retreated to a passageway in (C) Block behind the cells. As wounded officers had been rescued from the cell house, Warden Johnston decided it was time to put an end to the riot by re-taking the prison interior. At dawn a team of officers entered the cell house and proceeded slowly to (C) Block corridor. They quickly opened the door to the corridor and fired several rounds inside. They slammed the door and waited a couple of minutes, then repeated the process. Officers then entered the corridor and found the three inmates dead.

After two long days, the riot was finally over. The toll: two officers dead; 14 officers wounded; three inmates dead; one inmate wounded by marine grenades. Officer Stites died early in the riot while attempting to rescue Officer Burch in the West Gun Gallery. Officer Miller died later at Memorial Hospital as a result of being beaten and shot while a hostage.

Damage to the inside of the prison was in excess of one million dollars, most of which was caused by the marine grenades.

The remaining three ring leaders went on trial for first degree murder. All were found guilty. Inmates Thompson and Shockley were given the death penalty, and sent to San Quentin to await execution, while Carnes was given a life sentence tacked on to the ninety-nine years he was already serving.[3] Inmate Carnes was returned to Alcatraz from federal court and was placed in solitary confinement for seven years. Thompson and Shockley paid their debt to society in the gas chamber at San Quentin during December 1948, just over two and one half years after the riot.

There were several individual acts of heroism by officers during this bloody riot. By naming some of these officers, however, I would surely run the risk of forgetting someone. Therefore, I will defer to a statement made by Warden Johnston shortly after the riots conclusion. "All my officers did their duty—to a man."

---

[3] Clarence Carnes was paroled in 1973.

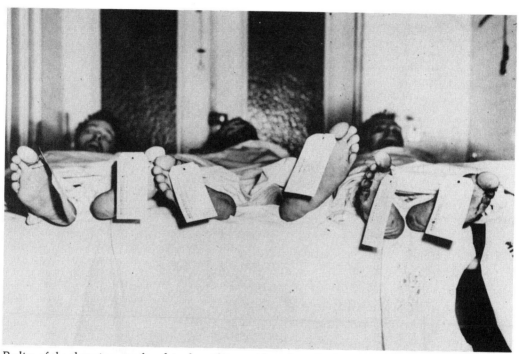

Bodies of the three inmates found in the utility corridor after officers recaptured the cellhouse. From left to right—Bernard Coy, Joseph Cretzer, and Marvin Hubbard. Courtesy of Golden Gate National Recreation Area.

BOAT SCHEDULE
Leaving Ft. Mason

Weekly	Saturday	Sunday	Holiday
A.M.	A.M.	A.M.	A.M.
12:25	12:25	12:25	12:25
6:55	7:10	7:10	7:10
7:30			
8:20	8:20	8:20	8:20
10:10	10:10	10:10	10:10
P.M.	P.M.	P.M.	P.M.
12:55	12:55	12:55	12:55
3:35	3:35	3:35	3:35
5:10	5:10	5:10	5:10
5:50	5:50	5:50	5:50
7:15	7:15	7:15	7:15
9:00	9:00	9:00	9:00
10:15	10:15	10:15	10:15
11:30	11:30	11:30	11:30

(Reverse Side Leaving Alcatraz)

BOAT SCHEDULE
Leaving Alcatraz

Weekly	Saturday	Sunday	Holiday
A.M.	A.M.	A.M.	A.M.
12:15	12:15	12:15	12:15
6:45	7:00	7:00	7:00
7:20			
8:10	8:10	8:10	8:10
10:00	10:00	10:00	10:00
P.M.	P.M.	P.M.	P.M.
12:45	12:45	12:45	12:45
3:25	3:25	3:25	3:25
5:00	5:00	5:00	5:00
5:40	5:40	5:40	5:40
7:00	7:00	7:00	7:00
8:45	8:45	8:45	8:45
10:00	10:00	10:00	10:00
11:15	11:15	11:15	11:15

(Reverse Side Leaving Ft. Mason)

Top: *Boat schedule leaving Alcatraz for Pier 4 and schedule leaving Fort Mason to Alcatraz.*

Bottom: *The Alcatraz Island launch "Warden Johnston." Courtesy of Edward Faulk.*

FIVE

The Prison Boats—
Lifeline To The Outside World

My father once told me that there were only four ways an inmate would ride the prison launch to San Francisco from Alcatraz Island. He would ride on the launch if he had to make a court appearance, was being transferred to another prison, or was released. The only other way he would take the boat trip was if he died.

During my eleven year residence on Alcatraz, very few were released. There were three reasons for this: 1. The number of inmates was small, so naturally there were fewer releases. 2. Even though 70% of the inmates transferred to Alcatraz were serving in excess of twenty five years, if they had served their time without problems, some would be transferred to other federal prisons. This factor alone, however, did not necessarily guarantee that they would be transferred. Several of Alcatraz's most famous inmates such as Capone, Kelly, and Stroud were transferred from the island for medical reasons. These men served a total of thirty-nine years on Alcatraz. The longest sentence served on "The Rock" by any one man was Alvin Karpis who's stay lasted over twenty-six years. 3. The Alcatraz Administration had decided early on that they would not release prisoners directly into the bay area community. This would eliminate any near by soap box to the press. The warden had decided that prior to an inmate's release he would be transferred to another federal prison. One must remember that from the beginning the San Francisco community was far from happy at the prospect of having some of America's most infamous criminals just a little over a mile from its shores.

One big event in my childhood years on Alcatraz was the transfer of inmates to and from the island. It was conducted in such a manner that there was never a burden placed on the routine function of the prison. By transferring inmates the way they did, the prison administration managed to keep the prisoner population fairly constant.

The transfer routine was invariably conducted as follows. All officers would receive word that a prisoner transfer was going to take place on a certain date. Thus, the island children would find out soon after the news broke. The procedure never varied. A special, non-scheduled boat was made ready to take prisoners off the island. This special boat would run between regularly scehduled boats and usually on weekends.

Approximately one hour prior to the boat's departure, several children and adults would line the balcony of 64 Building, which gave a full view of the dock, the boat ramp and boat itself. Within a few minutes a pick-up truck would arrive on the dock and park near the boat ramp. Personal affects of the inmates, such as a change of clothes, toilet articles, and maybe a musical instrument were taken from the truck and placed aboard the prison launch. A few minutes later two more pick-up trucks with canvas covers over them and bench seats would arrive from the prison. At this point there would be six or seven officers near the trucks. The officer in the dock tower, which was directly above, would oversee the entire operation.

Now, as all eyes were on the first truck, inmates began to file out. They were bound with wrist and ankle irons. A chain went from the ankle irons up to the wrist irons and passed through a waist holder and on to the next inmate. Each inmate's movement was severely limited by the chains. He could only shuffle about twelve inches at a time. After the first inmates were on the boat, the second group would repeat the process.

The prison launch, with several of the officers on board, would then proceed to Pier 4 in San Francisco, where it was met by Federal Marshals. The inmates were then loaded on a bus and taken to the train station to complete the final leg of their journey to another federal prison. The number of inmates that was transferred was usually twenty or twenty-two. This ritual usually occurred twice a year.

Within a month another special boat, with inmates, would arrive at the island

View of the dock area, boat ramp, and a small section of the dock tower. This is where island kids used to watch the chain gang style inmate transfers. Prison launch in the boat slip is the "McDowell". Picture taken in 1948. Courtesy of Edward Faulk.

from other federal prisons. Again, two trucks were waiting on the dock and when the inmates got off the boat they would be chained in the same manner as those who left the island earlier. The number of inmate arrivals were usually equal to the number transferred. As the newly arriving inmates left the boat, we could watch them look around trying to take in everything at once. No doubt they had heard many strange things prior to their arrival at the island. After loading they were driven up to the prison where they were processed and integrated into the main-stream prison population. I often wondered what went through the new inmates' minds as they got their first look at "The Rock". During my eleven years on the island I must have witnessed these human chain-gang style transfers at least eight times in each direction, both leaving and arriving. It should be noted however, that these federal prisoners differed considerably from the chain gangs of the old South. These inmates were hardened criminals who for one reason or another fouled up at some other federal prison. The prisoner was encouraged to serve his time "trouble free", so that within three to five years he might be transferred to another prison. The length of his stay, to a large extent, depended on his conduct.

Needless to say, witnessing the transfer of inmates as a young boy left a very deep impression on me. After over 30 years I can still picture the prisoner transfers as if they had occurred only yesterday.

A court appearance by an inmate would mean that he also had to be chained as described earlier, brought down to the launch and placed aboard. If only one inmate made an appearance, a special boat would not be scheduled. The prisoner would board before any residents of the island and upon arrival at Pier 4 in San Francisco he would disembark first. While making the boat trip to and from the mainland, the inmate would be isolated in a small cabin just behind the pilot house. This trip to court would probably have been the first time since arriving that the inmate had been off the island, so he tried to take in as much as he could. He observed the women, of course, but he also looked at cars, what people were wearing, etc. One of the reasons for these intense observations was that he knew when he returned to the island the other prisoners would expect him to fill them in on all that he had seen while away from the island.

A view of the Island's water barge and the prison launch "Warden Johnston." The barge carried all of the Island's fresh water. It could also transport different kinds of fuels in separate tanks as well as cargo. Notice the three windows with venetian blinds on board the prison launch. This cabin was used to transport inmates to court, etc. The warden also used the cabin whenever he was on board. Everyone else sat in the main cabin which is located to the rear of the two windows that face aft. The two cabins were separated by a wall and door. Courtesy of Golden Gate National Recreation Area.

There were several different boats and small ships that made Alcatraz a port of call for one reason or another, especially during the 1930's and 1940's.

The U.S. Army steamer *Frank M. Coxe* traveled between Fort Mason in San Francisco, to the *Presidio*, Angel Island, and finally onto Alcatraz, to either pick up laundry for the army or to leave dirty laundry. The *Coxe* also made a run to Alcatraz at 8:10 am to pick up school children and transport them to Pier 4. It would make a return trip with school children at 5:00 pm. After World War II when the laundry quota dropped off, the *Coxe* discontinued its Alcatraz run in early 1948. There were two U.S. Army water ships, the *El Equador* and the *El Aquario*, that made regular runs to Alcatraz. They were sister ships, which were approximately one hundred twenty feet long and carried several thousand gallons of water. The island had no fresh water of its own, so it had to be transported to a 250,000 gallon storage tank which was built in 1939. These two ships carried water to the island until 1947 at which time a large water barge belonging to the Army was leased to the island and took over that duty until the island closed.

When my family first moved to Alcatraz in 1942 the prison had only one launch. It was called the *McDowell* and was about fifty feet long. The launch had a seating capacity of just over forty people. Because the launch was getting on in age the prison administration requested a new boat. The plan was to use the new launch daily and keep the *McDowell* as a back up boat. The request was made to McNeil Island Federal Prison in Washington State in 1944. McNeil had the only boat yard in the federal prison system. The launch was named after the first warden of Alcatraz, Warden Johnston. It was constructed by McNeil Island prisoners, completed and commissioned in 1945, and delivered to Alcatraz shortly thereafter. The boat was presented to Warden Johnston by McNeil's warden, Paul Squier (the writer's uncle). The *Warden Johnston* was just over sixty-three feet long and could seat over fifty persons. It had a pilot house, private cabin just behind that and a large main cabin. It also seated some ten people outside on the fantail. The private cabin was used by the warden when he was aboard or for transporting inmates to court.

When the prison boat was ready to make a trip to the mainland, the officer assigned to the launch would approach the barbed wire fence that surrounded

A rare view of the U.S. Army Steamer General Frank M. Coxe *docked at Alcatraz in 1940. This dock was replaced in early 1940's by a much larger facility. (Note size of dock on page 51) Courtesy of Edward Faulk.*

the entire dock tower. After pressing a button to the tower, the tower officer would put the boat keys in a holder and lower them down to the waiting boat officer. The tower officer would then enter a notation in his log of who the keys were given to and at what time. The keys to the dock tower were transferred in the same manner when the officer on duty was relieved. The boat pilot was also responsible for keeping a log regarding all boat trips, no matter how routine.

When one observed just how cautiously this federal prison was operated, you found that good, consistent, routine procedures were the watch words of safety and successful function. It can not be stressed too often to the reader that Alcatraz Island was a maximum security prison with the emphasis on maximum. It was us kids that somehow managed to circumvent the rules always careful to walk that fine line between bending and outright breaking island regulations. In retrospect I believe our mischief was more growing pains than anything else. Nothing we did as children was of a malicious nature.

A view of the dock and waiting room on Pier 4 at Fort Mason. All scheduled prison boats docked here. Looking at the extreme right center of the picture the reader can just see the bow of the Frank M. Coxe. *Courtesy of Golden Gate National Recreation Area.*

Photograph of the writer on the lower balcony of "Old 64 Building."
About thirty feet behind the balcony turns left and overlooks the
dock. This was our first home on the island. (Picture taken 1944)

SIX

Growing Up On Alcatraz—Part I

I think the title of this chapter can be summarized in about six words—a very different kind of childhood.

Let me start at the beginning and first tell you how I arrived at my home on Alcatraz Island, and a little something about my family. My father and mother were married in 1924; that same year my father took a position as a Federal Correctional Officer at McNeil Island Federal Prison in Washington. He spent sixteen years working at this penitentiary, the first six years living on the island. In 1930 they moved to Tacoma, Washington, and my father commuted to the island. My brother and I were both born in Tacoma.

In 1940 my father was transferred to Terminal Island Federal Prison near Long Beach, California. In late 1941 he was once again transferred, this time to the Federal Prison at La Tuna, Texas; so we packed up and went to live in Texarkana, Arkansas. After a few months my father received orders he was to be transferred to Alcatraz Island. The family moved to San Francisco in July, 1942. There was no housing available on the island, so we rented an apartment in San Francisco until we were able to move onto the island. With the war on, It was hard to find a place to live.

During the remainder of that summer my father commuted to and from the island. Finally he arrived home one day and announced that we had been offered housing and were moving to Alcatraz.

The night before we moved I must admit that sleep deserted me. I was very excited about the prospect of living on Alcatraz Island. I was also a little frightened. After all we were not moving to some housing project where we would be

59

A view of "Old 64 Building" overlooking the dock area. This impressive structure was built by the U.S. Army in 1905 and was the sight of my first home on Alcatraz. The building along with the dock watch tower at right are still standing today. Note the main watch tower on top of the prison building. Courtesty of San Francisco Public Library.

allowed to move about and go anywhere at anytime we wished. My father told my brother and me that our lives would be very restricted.

My mother's reaction to the move, I suppose, was one of a typical mother who would be glad to settle in one place for a little while and get some stability in our lives. I rather doubt if there was much apprehension on my mother's part about actually moving onto the island. After all, she lived on McNeil Island for years, sometimes alone for a week at a time while my father was out with a group of officers and dogs on a manhunt to recapture escaped inmates. Her nearest neighbor was sometimes three to five miles away. I do believe, though, that she may have had some second thoughts about raising two boys in a very confined area, which just happened to be a maximum security prison. The next morning we drove to the foot of Van Ness Avenue, parked the car after unloading our belongings, and waited for the launch. After a twelve minute boat ride to the island we unloaded our furniture on the dock with a lot of help from island residents. The whole family was ushered to the dock office by way of a full-body metal detector. After walking through the detector, we were directed to a counter at the side of the office. My father filled out some papers, then he was given a set of island rules and regulations and the boat schedule. After this was completed, we were escorted to our new home. As we walked up the stairway from the dock, my eyes tried to take in everything at once. I must say that the island looked forbidding to a small boy. There were gun towers with officers, cement, rock, and stone wherever you looked. Our first home on Alcatraz was located on the lower balcony of a three story structure known as 64 Building. It was built one year before the San Francisco earthquake of 1906 and housed military guards and their dependents. The building itself was and still is an impressive structure of gray stone overlooking the island dock facilities and facing a fifty foot high dock tower, which was manned 24 hours a day.

64 Building was not only home for approximately twenty-five families, but also housed a very well stocked market called "the canteen". A shopper was able to purchase almost any item that could be obtained from a small market in San Francisco. Adjacent to the canteen was the post office. This post office was first located at the other end of 64 Building, but after World War II it was moved nearer the canteen for convenience.

61

Hoisting a 40 millimeter anti-aircraft gun on top of the B & C building during World War II. Courtesy of Golden Gate National Recreation Area.

I will never forget one day as a small boy walking into the old war time post office for the first time. There on the wall was a poster of Uncle Sam. He had steel blue eyes and they stared at you no matter where you walked in the room, and a pointed finger that did the same. The caption on top of the poster read, "Uncle Sam wants you." I finally convinced myself after a couple of visits to the post office that at my tender age and even with the war in full swing he (Uncle Sam) could not have possibly wanted me for anything!

The housing in Building 64 was not luxurious by any standards. The ceilings were twelve feet high and looked about thirty to me. The floors were uneven, and heat was provided by steam radiators. Electricity was direct current from huge generators located in the power house building. During the forties this was just fine as most small appliances were either a.c. or d.c. Sometime later, however, when we purchased our first television set, we had to also buy a converter. The set was plugged into the converter to change the current from d.c. to a.c. in order to prevent the straight d.c. current from blowing our t.v. out.

My brother Chuck was nine years old when we moved on to the island. Being the typical younger brother and not knowing any of the other kids, I did the normal thing younger brothers do; I tagged along after him, sticking very close. As we both got acquainted with other children nearer our ages, we began to make our own friends. My brother and I did, however, remain close while living on the island and until Chuck went off to college in 1951. After my father retired in 1953, my brother and I left home, and we pursued different careers. Since 1985 though, we live within twenty miles and see each other fairly often.

My father had many different assignments on Alcatraz, such as one of the five towers, kitchen detail, cell blocks, gun armory, prison work shops, etc. As a small boy I did not give much thought to what my father did on the island, however, as I grew older I came to realize that he, like the other officers, had a very dangerous job, especially here on Alcatraz. After all, this island was considered the prison bureau's ultra maximum security penitentiary. He was well liked by his fellow officers, and from all I have heard, he was respected by most of the inmates, as much as they respected any officer.

Life changed for me in several ways by moving onto the island. As I stated

The 40 millimeter anti-aircraft gun pictured on page 62 in place on the roof with its Army gun crew. Courtesy of Golden Gate National Recreation Area.

earlier, there were several rules and regulations. Everyone knew the rules were set down for security reasons, and the restrictions were tough. I learned immediately that officers' dependents were restricted to less than four acres of the twelve acre island. The restricted area was separated by a ten foot high fence with barbed wire on top. Dependents were allowed to move freely on the south east portion of the island with two exceptions. One was access to the dock. In order to take the prison launch to San Francisco, you first were stopped by an electrically operated gate, which blocked the stairway that led to the dock. This fence was controlled by the officer in the dock tower. He had visual contact with anyone who pressed the button to pass. After he recognized the person as an officer or dependent, he would trip the lock and allow passage. The second rule mainly applied to children under sixteen years. They were not allowed on any part of the beach for any reason. After 5:00 pm on weekdays and on weekends, adults could fish in certain areas of the beach and the dock. No one could fish however, while prisoners were working away from the prison till 5:00 pm on weekdays.

The boat schedule was the one thing all new residents memorized very quickly, as this was their ticket to the outside world. You could not just pick up a phone and order a cab or catch a bus at the corner. First of all there was only one outside line from the island to the rest of the world, and it was located "up top" in the prison administration building. This was the #1 phone. Within five years of moving to the island, a second outside line was installed. This was in a phone booth located on the balcony of Building 64. The third phone to the outside was a sit down phone booth located in the hallway of (B) Building, or the "new apartments" situated on the southwest corner of the island. The last two phones were located in buildings where dependents lived.

The #1 phone was for official business mostly and could only be used on a personal basis in emergency cases. The #2 and #3 phones could be used by all dependents. The last two phones were a big morale booster to families on the island.

There was also an inter-island phone system. These phone numbers were contained in a small pamphlet-type phone directory and were located at all officer duty stations such as towers, dock, shops, dining hall, etc. Every family also had this phone directory.

65

Alcatraz Island children walking down to the dock to catch the morning boat for school. Courtesy of Golden Gate National Recreation Area.

School children boarding the prison launch Warden Johnston at 3:35 pm from pier 4 in San Francisco on their return trip home to Alcatraz. Courtesy of San Francisco Public Library.

The first time my brother and I ventured out into the area we were allowed to be in, we made several observations. First, there was only one large tree for climbing on the south end of the island, and it was located outside the cliff wall (out of bounds for small kids—at least for a little while). Secondly, we noticed some army soldiers playing basketball on the side of the handball court. We asked them what the army was doing on the island. One of them stepped out from behind the building and pointed to the roof of the new apartments, B and C Building. There, on top of the roof, was a 40 millimeter anti aircraft ak-ak gun. The men told us that just after Pearl Harbor they (six of them) were assigned to the island for protection of the bay area, and Alcatraz in particular from enemy aircraft. They lived in a roof apartment adjacent to the gun. They remained on the island almost to the end of the war. The third thing that I noticed right away was that there were no animals, like dogs or cats, on the island, that I could see. When I asked my father about this he told me the island was too small for most animals, but that we could own a hamster or a small turtle. I had two turtles while on the island.

Actually there were dogs on the island. I remember two. The first one in the mid-forties was a little black Scotty dog that belonged to the doctor. The other dog belonged to Warden Swope, who was warden from 1948 until 1955. He had a lovely Irish setter named "Pat". The children were never allowed near him and could only see him running around his yard at the side and rear of the warden's house, which was located "up top" next to the prison.

As we arrived on the island in early September, the first thing my mother had to do was enroll my brother and me in school. So one day my brother and I, along with my mother, took our first boat ride from the island to Pier 4 in San Francisco. On a nice day it was a very pleasant ride, and as I stated before, it took about twelve minutes for the crossing. We walked to the end of the pier and found our car where we had left it parked at the foot of Van Ness Street. (All private vehicles belonging to the families were left parked in San Francisco, as the island was not big enough to accommodate private cars.) We drove a little more than a mile up Van Ness, then turned right for one block to Sherman Grade School. Several of the island kids went to Sherman. After enrolling my brother in the fourth grade and me in the second, my mother was told that we

The prison launch "Warden Johnston" making a trip to Pier 4 in San Francisco. The ride took about twelve minutes. Courtesy of Edward Faulk.

The island canteen (store) where you could buy just about anything a small market had to offer. Courtesy of Golden Gate National Recreation Area.

would have to walk to school from the dock and back again each day as gas rationing was in effect due to the war.

As school would start in a few days, my mother took us shopping for clothes. Then we headed back to the foot of Van Ness Street, parked the car, walked back down the pier and waited for the boat to pick us up along with some other passengers.

Just a word about the vehicles that were on the island: they were all working vehicles (trucks) of one kind or another. There was a fire truck, a garbage truck, later a bus, a one ton flat bed truck and three canvas covered pick-up trucks. Most of these vehicles were kept on the dock at night. The keys were locked in a cabinet in the dock office with access by the Lt. (not that an inmate was going any place even if he got access to a vehicle.)

Well, the time came and school finally started. There were really two school boats in the morning for the kids. Junior and high school kids took the 7:20 am boat, because they had further to go, while the grade school kids who had a shorter distance would take the 8:10 am boat. Most of the kids would return to the island on the 3:35 pm boat.

A typical day for one in grade school would be as follows:

a) Get up about 7:00 am and do the usual things a grade school child does.
b) Get your lunch or lunch money (as there was no going home) and get any books or material you will need for the entire day (there's no returning home to pick up anything.)
c) Make sure you got down to the boat dock at least five minutes before the boat was ready to leave. It waited for no one but the warden.
d) When the boat leaves the island you could talk, but excessive noise would catch a quick reprimand from the boat officer. At least once a month, usually on a friday morning, both school boats would have a life jacket drill. The boat officer would demonstrate the correct way to put on a life jacket, then the children would have to do the same.

After arriving at Pier 4 and disembarking, the kids who went to the same school would team up and start walking. There was not much time for playing around as school started at nine o'clock, and you had to keep moving to make it. At school the group would split up and go with their own grades, but at the end of the day (3:00 pm) the kids quickly formed up and started out for the dock over a mile away. They had to move even faster than in the morning as they had to be at the dock by 3:35 pm. I am still amazed that some of the island children did not grow up to be cross country speed walkers.

Once back on the island all the kids would stop off at the "canteen" and have a coke and a candy bar. Then it was off to our own individual homes to change out of school clothes, and then meet somewhere to play together for about an hour until it was time for dinner. I will talk later in this chapter about some of the games we played on the island that were unique to our environment. There was a curfew on the island for anyone under sixteen years. This did not apply to me at my age, because by dark the wind picked up and the cold fog started rolling in, so in those first years the routine of being home early was the rule not the exception.

One of the first things I found to enjoy after arriving on the island was to sit on a bench which faced the channel looking towards San Francisco; it was located at the top of the path which leads to the beach. I would watch the large military ships come and go by the hour, for it was World War II, and the harbor was always teeming with activity. As the ships passed by this great city, it was as if they were saluting her while saying hello or goodbye. During the war the lights of the city were darkened, as I suppose they were up and down the coast, for security reasons.

The weather on Alcatraz Island was usually very predictable. It made very little difference what season of the year it was, as the fog would roll in from the Golden Gate almost on cue. It was pushed on its way by the winds most every day about dusk. Within an hour the two fog horns (one at each end of the island) would begin blasting away. Even with the wind blowing, the fog got so thick you could only see for a few yards. Occasionally, evening boat trips were canceled because of the fog. Sometimes even daytime boat trips were eliminated due to high winds and rough waters. When this occurred, all the school kids were a very happy group. The children usually missed about five days every school year due to weather conditions. Because the fog horns would sound the vast majority of the nights each year, I would find it hard to sleep sometimes when they were not blowing. I knew the sound of every fog horn in the bay area. I recall that on

Sign at south/west end of island stating "CABLE CROSSING – DO NOT ANCHOR". Kids hid behind the sign while prison launch was enroute to or from San Francisco. Note path which led down to the beach. Courtesy of San Francisco Public Library.

a few occasions when the two prison launches were gone from the island for an extended period of time such as maintenance, repairs, etc., the U.S. Army would lend the prison a boat for that period of time. This launch, called the *Countess* was about 50 feet long, but could seat only about thirty-five people. The *Countess* was very old and just about every time she made the crossing to and from the island, there was a certain amount of apprehension by most of the passengers.

One afternoon when most of the school children were returning home, we had boarded the *Countess* on a fairly foggy day. By 4:05 pm we were just clearing the end of Fort Mason Pier 2, when suddenly the fog was so thick you could not see from one end of the boat to the other. This was the kind of day even the Coast Guard would not go out in. I am not sure we had a very good compass, as we seemed to stop every couple of minutes to listen for the island fog horn. We arrived at the island after 6:00 pm. It was the longest boat trip I had ever made in either direction while living on Alcatraz. It took over two hours to go just under one and one-half miles. Well, at least we got home safely.

I did not get a chance to see the outside of the prison up close until Christmas Eve 1942. It was an island tradition that all the children, under the direction of an adult, went Christmas caroling each year. The children would gather on the lower balcony of 64 Building overlooking the dock. When the 7:00 pm boat would return to the island, all the children would begin to sing. After a few minutes the group would move onto various stops throughout the residential areas, sing a couple of carols, then proceed on. At 8:00 pm we were let through the restricted gate on the southwest end of the island. We would climb the hill leading to the warden's house "up top". On the way, we passed near the southwest part of the prison which contains inmates in (D) Block. These were the hardcore inmates in solitary confinement. As our closest point to the prison now was only about 100 feet, we stopped and sang a couple of carols. Then all the children would yell "Merry Christmas" to the inmates. Within a few seconds many shouts of a similar nature would echo back. This same event would happen every year, and each year I thought that our happiest night must have been one of their saddest.

We next moved to the top of the hill where a complex of buildings were located, including the Prison Administration, the warden's home, lighthouse, and the doctor's home. All the children gathered outside Warden Johnston's house and began singing. The Warden and Mrs. Johnston would step outside and listen for a few minutes, and then Mrs. Johnston would invite us all into their home for hot drinks, cookies, and other assorted goodies.

As the warden's house was adjacent to the prison itself, I got my first chance to get a close up view of the exterior of this large cream colored building. Because it was almost always foggy "up top", and this night was no exception, I got a very eerie feeling with the fog horns blowing and the lighthouse beacon piercing through the night.

Although officers and their families were transferred to and from the island periodically, I did make friends with three boys my age, and these friendships lasted until I left the island. Even though there were several girls on the island, at this point in my life they were not in the picture. One day a friend of mine asked me if I had been down to the beach yet. I told him no. He said that he and some of the other boys would go down every weekend to search for things which had washed ashore as a result of World War II. He talked about finding military rations and waterproof boxes containing milk chocolate, cigarettes, etc. So, the next weekend four of us sneaked down the pathway to the beach, which is located on the southwest corner of the island and faces directly towards San Francisco. We searched around for quite sometime when one of my friends looked up and realized the prison launch was on its way back from the mainland. One of the boys said, "follow me," so we all ran to the end of the beach and started up the path. About one third of the way up we ducked down behind a large sign, and stayed there until the boat had rounded the island and headed for the dock. My heart was in my throat. What if someone on the boat had seen us? Several days passed and nothing happened, so I knew we were home free. I later found out that the sign we hid behind read, "Cable Crossing—Do Not Anchor." I was to hide behind that sign many times in the years to come. We made many more trips down to the beach and were often successful in our salvaging efforts. We also became much more careful of when the boat was due, even though we still ended up behind the sign board once in a while.

We were not yet allowed inside the hand ball court (gym), so we played a lot of basketball along side the building. As the whole area around the residence on the south end of the island was cement, we asked our fathers if they would request prison officials to paint a baseball diamond near the new apartments and the security fence. Much to our surprise, a detail (two inmates and an officer) showed up a few days later and painted a baseball diamond right where we wanted it.

After the war ended, some things changed for my group. We were now able to take the boat over to San Francisco and go downtown on the street car by ourselves to see the Saturday matinee. The years following World War II and before the Korean War broke out, were good years on the island for a kid growing up. First, in 1947 we were allowed to have bicycles on the island. There was not a lot of room to ride, as we had to stay in the area of the large and little parade grounds, (open spaces surrounded by residences used for marching, parades, etc., when Alcatraz was under the military).

A cement floor was poured in the outer room of the handball court, and we were allowed to keep our bicycles in it. The inner door leading to the gym as well as the ladder, which led up to the second floor table tennis room, were locked and off limits to kids under fourteen years. Other things were happening about this time. The prison authorities began showing 16mm travelogues by Standard Oil Company for the residents about twice a month. These films were shown atop (C) Building in a large room called the solarium. In 1948 a few movies were shown to dependents in the prison chapel. This practice was discontinued for security reasons. A projection room was completed and the movies were moved to the social hall on the east side of the island. We will talk about the social hall and the handball court in the next chapter as a good portion of my teen-age years were tied to these buildings.

There were some things that were typical of any young boy growing up, whether it was on Alcatraz or any place else. I remember having a turtle called "Junior" right after the war ended. One summer day about a year after I got him, Junior died. I put him in a large stick match box and sneaked over the cliff to bury him. I had to do this because there was very little dirt on the legal side of the wall. After I found the perfect spot for Junior, I buried him. Afterwards, I must have sat there for two hours crying my eyes out. I felt like I had lost my best friend. About a month later I returned to the area where I had buried Junior just to see how he was doing, but I couldn't find him. As I think back now, it was probably just as well.

As I said earlier, I wanted the reader to have some idea of the games we played on the island that were unique to our environment. The children were not allowed to play with or have in their possession any type of toy guns, knives, etc., not even if they were rubber. So we had to come up with our own games. We never played cowboys and Indians like most kids. The most popular game we played was called "Guards and Cons". About three kids would be cons and five would be guards. We had the perfect prison, which was between an apartment and one of the island's natural rock walls. To the rear of this ten foot by twenty-five foot enclosed area, was a forty foot high, chain link fence. The guards had to stand behind a certain point. A con would start to climb the fence. If the guard could not get up to the fence fast enough to tag him, then there was an escape. The escaped con could only hide in 64 Building and once he found a place to hide he had to stay there. The guards (usually two for one escape) would have one half hour to find him. Of course, everyone wanted to be a con.

As I mentioned before, the large parade ground was a big expanse of cement (about two acres) surrounded by residences on three sides and the security fence on the fourth side. During the thirties, cement had been poured for a tennis court that was no longer in use. This was the perfect place for all the kids to roller skate, and we became quite good. We played a game called "One foot off the gutter". I grant you, not a very classy title, but nevertheless a unique game of skill. The way it worked was simple. One kid was "it" or in the center between the two tennis poles by himself (no net of course). As skaters would try to get past him, the "it" person in the middle would try to tag him. If he succeeded, then the person tagged would have to stay in the center and keep tagging others. The more people that got tagged, the harder it was for the skaters who were trying not to get caught. Finally the last skater left would be the winner.

As I look back on those early days of my childhood on Alcatraz so many, many years ago, I think now that life was made more exciting merely because of the place where we lived. However, I knew that all the children of Alcatraz carried with them the constant knowledge that, although we had a lot of fun playing different games, it could very well be a life and death game at any time up at the prison. The '46 Riot was still fresh in everyone's mind.

There were two other activities I should mention before we move on. The canteen (store) used to put out their empty orange crates and stack them to the side of the building. From the little parade ground down to the side of the canteen was a fifty step stairway. Normally this would only be a twenty-five step stairway, but many of the stairways on Alcatraz were constructed this way. The reason for the tiny steps was quite ingenious. If an inmate escaped and started running down the stairs, the chances that he would fall and break his neck were fairly good. I fell on them often just taking two at a time. Anyway, because of these small steps the staircase made a perfect ride. We would take one of the orange crates and knock out the center divider. Then one boy would sit in it at the top of the stairs, while someone gave him a push. I don't have to tell you this was a scary ride. Speeds could get up to about fifteen miles per hour. The stairs were narrow enough that you could not go sideways. As you got to the end of the stairway you had to come up running because the orange crate would disintegrate upon impact at the bottom of the stairs.

A lot of people would say we were nuts to do things like this, but I believe when you live in a highly restricted environment you dream up things to do. It is possibly true that only a kid would do something like this. I know that now I would not go down those stairs for a million dollars.

One other game (and I use the word loosely) we played was located over the cliff. The area from the path to the beach and the fog horn were the boundaries. This was an area of about a block and a half long and seventy-five to one hundred feet wide. The island had different varieties of ice plants, one of which had flowers in them. Just before they bloomed they were in the form of small, hard pod. We would pick them at this stage and load up our pockets with them. Then we would choose up sides and each team would go in opposite directions. Then each group would search the other out and have a fight by throwing these little green things at each other. They hurt when you got hit, even though most of the kids would wear two pairs of pants, a heavy coat, plus some kind of hat. I don't believe anyone ever won.

Tunnel/roadway running the length of 64 Building on its west side. Built in 1866. The bomb shelter is located here. It was called "Chinatown." Courtesy of Golden Gate National Recreation Area.

I remember one time lying on the roof of the fog horn during one of these "war games" as we called them. It was a bright sunny day, and I could see couple of the other team kids sneaking along just below me. All of a sudden the fog horn sounded with a deafening blast, and scared me so bad I almost fell off the roof and down the cliff. I knew that the coast guard did test the two island fog horns occasionally, but the timing was sure off as far as I was concerned! Oh well, there would be other days and games.

Then there was the time a few in our group decided to try smoking. One of the kids took a pack of cigarettes from a carton his mother had. The only problem was where to go and smoke them. As we were still fairly young and the war had only been over about a year, we decided to go to the island bomb shelter. The shelter was located in 64 Building below ground level in a tunnel-like area. It was built by the army in 1866. It was commonly referred to as "Chinatown" by the kids. There was no problem getting into the shelter, because it had been unlocked since the war began. Inside there were six or seven army cots with blankets and mattresses. This was the perfect place to smoke, or so we thought. After we lit our cigarettes, had a few puffs, and started getting more and more dizzy, someone dropped a lit cigarette on one of the bunks. After a few minutes the blanket and then the mattress began smoldering. Smoke started to fill the room. We all began to panic. We did, however, manage to find a fire extinguisher and empty it onto the blanket and mattress. Then we took both outside and jumped up an down on them till we thought they were completely out. We left them outside and decided to return in a couple of hours to make sure they were both out, especially the mattress. In a couple of hours two of us did go back and found that everything was all right. We put the blanket and mattress back in the bomb shelter and left, hoping that no one would see the evidence of our misdeeds for some time to come. Our luck held as our little indiscretion was not discovered for approximately two months. At once, the shelter was secured and remained that way until the island was closed. The result at that time was a memo to all officers with families.

The only other time I was in the bomb shelter was shortly after my family moved onto the island. As World War II was about one year old in 1942, and the outcome was still in doubt, every family had in their pamphlet of rules and

One of the two fog horns on the island. This one is located on the south/west end of the island. Note century plants and Golden Gate Bridge in the background. Courtesy of Phil Palmer.

regulations a section on what to do in case there was an air raid. The rules stated that if an air attack should occur, the prison whistle would blow in a pattern every thirty seconds for fifteen seconds (this whistle was entirely different from the escape siren). Well, apparently one of the coast watchers along the beaches of San Francisco thought he saw one or more unidentified planes, so he called it in to his superiors. Within a few minutes I was on my way to the bomb shelter in my pajamas, as it was between 9:00 and 10:00 pm, and I was just seven years old. As we all raced to the bomb shelter, it became apparent that everyone was not going to fit into the shelter. As I recall, most all the women and children did get inside; however, several of the men (off-duty) had to stand outside. Fortunately, this air raid turned out to be a false alarm (no pun intended).

In 1947 my family moved into the "new apartments" in (C) Building. This building was completed in 1940 and was modern even by today's standards. They had three bedrooms, low ceilings, pegged wood floors, and stainless steel sinks. Twelve of the apartments in the building had open balconies that faced towards the big parade ground, while the remaining six apartments had enclosed balconies which faced San Francisco. All the apartments, however, gave a spectacular view of the city. I believe that the rent was just $47.50 per month.

I will talk about special days on the island each year, but here I would like to relate one yearly ritual. At Christmas time the family would all go to the city to pick out a tree. Once that was done, the ordeal began. We would drive down to the dock and unload the tree along with about ten others. Keep in mind that nearly fifty-five families were doing the same thing within about a week's time. Each owner tagged his own tree, and placed it on top of the boat cabin securing it as best he could. Then he would hope that during the crossing to the island the tree would not get blown into the water. Once on the island my father had to carry the tree up the steps, along the balcony of 64 Building and then across the almost always windy big parade ground. Eventually we all arrived home with the tree minus a few branches and some bent ones. Every year my father would say the same thing. He was going to invent a two inch tree that he could carry in his pocket. When he got home he would water it and then it would grow to normal size. After we got the tree all decorated, the trouble of getting it home would soon be forgotten.

A letter written by my Grandmother to my Mother in March 1950. The pelican mark, designated "Alcatraz Landing" and the mark designated "Alcatraz," both originated in the nineteenth century. Both were official Alcatraz cancellation marks.

One of the nicest things that took place on the island was my grandmother's yearly visit from Los Angeles. She would always spend two weeks. She was certainly quite a lady. When she arrived on the plane at San Francisco Airport, the whole family was expected to be there to greet her. Even though she was seventy years old, she was very independent, living by herself in the heart of downtown Los Angeles. She always took the champagne flight and was the last one off the plane. If her hat was a little crooked from a couple of champagnes, no one would dare say anything. She would hug and kiss everyone, then dash off through the terminal so fast that no one could keep up with her. I must tell you that no grass grew under her feet!

We had previously made arrangements with prison officials for her two week stay, so we would have no trouble getting her over to the island. My grandmother loved to play the horses in the daily paper, for up to a nickel a race. My brother, who was fourteen by now, was the banker. We all played except my father. You could only bet on a horse to win. When you got the newspaper on tuesday (no racing on monday) everyone would look over the entries and then make their bets. When wednesday's newspaper arrived, you would get the results. Imagine, a bookie operation right on Alcatraz Island! I am afraid we were very small fry, especially playing with our own money. Why sometimes the pot could get all the way up to 30 or 40 cents!

There was an older boy on the island who handled all four of the San Francisco papers. The morning papers would arrive on the 6:30 am boat. He would rush around delivering them and then catch the 7:20 am boat for school. In the afternoon, when he got home, he would deliver the evening papers that came over on the same boat (3:35 pm) that he did. I think that just about all of the fifty-five families on the island subscribed to a newspaper in those days, before t.v. became such a big part of every day life.

I would usually try and stay home from school at least one day while my grandmother was there. If it was one of the wind swept rainy days on the island, she would make the two of us tea with crackers and butter. We would sit at the kitchen table and lookout over the big parade ground, just watching the rain. Every once in a while someone would make a dash from one location to another. I was always sorry to see her visit come to an end.

During the long summer days when it was hard to find something to do, a couple of us boys would go to the canteen (store), and pick up two thirty-two ounce bottles of either 7-up or ginger ale. Then we would go home get a sandwich and then sneak over the cliff to the "sundeck". The "sundeck" was a six foot by six foot ledge carved out of the cliff. No one ever had any idea who went to all the trouble for a sundeck, but most of the kids made good use of it. It was located about half way between the cliff wall and the area where the cliff makes a sheer drop to the beach. The deck was just behind (B) Building off the big parade ground. When we arrived at the sundeck we would punch a hole in the top of each bottle with a nail (they were not easy to find on the island), then we would shake them up and blast each other until we were a mess. We usually spent the afternoon there watching the sea gulls fly by, trying to make some progress against the wind. Another nice thing about the sundeck was that the prison launch could not see us either going to the mainland or returning to the island. All we had to do was lay flat until the boat was too far away to see while enroute to the mainland. When it retuned to the island, we waited until it rounded the end and disappeared from view.

I remember the foggy nights on the island. We would go to the canteen and wait for shoppers to leave. When it was very foggy and dark, we would try to follow them from the store until they got home. We would see just how close we could get to them. If they heard something and turned around, we quickly ducked into the nearest doorway. Sometimes we got caught, but other times we were able to follow someone all the way home.

Probably one of the more scary things that we did was to take our worn out skate wheels and build a wooden cart. We would then put the wheels on the cart and attach a steering wheel on it so we could turn. Most kids everywhere do the same. The different thing about our cart was that we would mount a broomstick in front of the cart and then attach part of a sheet to it, for a makeshift sail. We then rolled it out on a very windy day by the old tennis court where we always skated. When the wind began blowing very hard the cart was let go with one and sometimes two kids on it. There were a couple of problems. One was that before you knew it, you were going about twenty miles per hour, and the cliff wall would be coming up quick. This meant you had to turn right fairly soon. If you were successful and made the turn you could roll past the cottages all the way to the area of the path that leads down to the beach. If you did not make the turn, you had a small problem. Fortunately, we made the turn most of the time. I repeat, most of the time. Seldom, if ever, did we miss the turn, as the alternative was to smash headlong into the rock wall.

All in all, the children on the island lived a fairly normal life. One must remember that our activities were dictated by where we lived and by the restrictions we lived under. Then there was the overriding fact that after all we were just kids.

We did all the normal things like trade comic books and baseball cards, just like kids do today. During World War II we saved our dimes and quarters until we had $18.75 so we could turn them in for a $25.00 savings bond. I believe our childhood years on Alcatraz were fairly normal. After all, where else would a kid be restricted from going to a beach. Freedom of movement was about the hardest thing a growing boy had to live with on the island. As I reminisce now, I realize the most exciting times of my childhood were still in the future.

Photograph taken of the writer near the South/West corner of the big parade ground. To my left is the Captain's house and in the distance a cottage and "Old 64 Building". (Picture taken in 1947)

SEVEN

Growing Up On Alcatraz—Part II

Since leaving Alcatraz Island, people have asked me one question more than any other. Did children who lived on the island have any contact with the inmates? The answer is yes. I read an article recently on the history of the island. It was a near factual article on Alcatraz, but it stated categorically that children never came in contact with or talked to the inmates. The reality was that we not only saw inmates, but talked to them on several occasions.

There were many times when inmates were around the different residential areas for one resason or another. Some would be assigned to clean-up details, garbage detail or dropping off the laundry. We did not stand around passing the time of day with them. However, there was one inmate that we (most of the kids) talked to for extended periods of time. We shall call this inmate Pickett. Every saturday and sunday he was allowed to tend the flower garden located near the warden's and chief medical officer's homes. On sunday mornings he would pick several bunches of flowers. He then put them in cans of water, and under the supervision of an officer, was allowed to bring them down to the gate at the security fence near the little parade ground. Every sunday the kids would wait for Pickett to arrive so they could pick up flowers for their mothers. In the couple of years that I participated in this flower program, I must have learned Pickett's life story. He was serving life and forty years for murder and various other crimes. He had spent almost all of his adult life in custody. He was a man of about forty-five years at that time. I don't know what happened to him, as I left the island before he did.

Obtaining flowers for your home every so often was nice, because the warden's garden was the only place where flowers (except wild) were grown. Keep in mind that the other name for the place was "The Rock". There were few places where things grew except on the side of the cliff. That was just about the only place on the island that had an abundance of dirt.

I remember when I lived in Building 64. The inmates would come around on clean-up details. Again, we would exchange pleasantries and then go about our business. It was the same on the garbage truck and especially on the laundry detail. The prison did all the dependents' laundry, and they would deliver it in heavy brown paper. After just a little bit of work you could make a very strong kite out of that paper. Of course, with all the heavy winds on the island, you would have to add at least twenty feet of tail and then hook it all up to your fishing rod and reel with its twenty-five pound test line. Then you were ready to go fly your kite.

As you can see in the photograph of me at the beginning of this chapter, to my left is a little patch of grass adjacent to the captain's house. It actually measured about fifty feet long by twenty-five feet wide. This was by far the largest area of grass on the island except for an identical patch along side the associate's house. We knew that the captain would be working during the day so several of us would use the grass for a slow motion football game. This may not be the most effective way to play football, but as we were dealing with such a small area, we had to come up with creative solutions. We were probably kicked off this grass at least a hundred times, but like a bad penny—well, I am sure the reader understands.

At about this time I began going steady with the Captain's youngest daughter, whom I will call Joan. I never was the apple of the captain's eye. I don't think it was anything personal, he was just a protective father. But as this was my first true love, I overlooked the captain's doubts about me, and the fact that I am sure he would liked to have wrung my neck, or worse. I remember once when I was in Southern California I bought a little ring ($3 maybe) and had my initials put on it. When I got back to the island I gave it to Joan, but I remember telling her not to let her father see it. At this time, 1950, most guys were giving their girls' big rings they could wear on a chain around their necks. That would have been good because every time we would have a fight (argument) she would take off the ring, tell me we were through, and then give it a pitch. When she did this we were often in the area of her house on the big parade ground and it was usually dark. It always ended the same way. We would make up, she would go into the house and get a flashlight, and then we would spend the next couple of hours looking for that ring. I never did understand why we could not break-up once in a while during the day time.

During this period (late 1950), we were able to get into the handball court (gym) once in a while. We played a lot of basketball, volley ball and table tennis. I was fairly good at the first two, but I must admit there were a couple of girls in our group who must have taken table tennis lessons in Red China. Most of the guys were embarrassed to play them. These same two girls were great volley ball players also, It was really something because as soon as a game was over they both would turn right back into girls again (amazing)!

Now that I was in my teen years, things seemed like they were coming together. In our island group, there were about eight boys and ten girls, so you always had a dancing partner. Some times a girl or boy would decide to date a boy or girl from the city (San Francisco). This usually did not work out because the person who lived on the island was always concerned with catching a boat. It was very awkward to have a boy friend or girlfriend visit you on the island (except for a big dance), because of the red tape for the visitor to get on the island, and then there was the ever present boat schedule. I recall whenever we had a dance at the social hall, the boat schedule always interfered as guests were coming and going, and working around the schedule.

There were a couple of bits of mischief the boys used to get into. Once we were given the key to the handball court by the officer in charge. As we felt that we were certainly old enough to have access to the gym anytime we wanted, we simply kept the key, and then told him we could not find it. The next day when we were in the city, we had five keys made, returned the original key to the officer, and told him we had found the key.

Now let me tell you about one more of our adventures, which came very close to backfiring on us. One of the main sources of entertainment for us was the social hall. If we could get a chaperon, we could hold dances on friday or saturday nights, but it was not always easy to accomplish this. The hall also had two pool tables and two bowling lanes.

The only problem was that the social hall was located over a block inside the security fence. Some of the guys felt that playing pool was about the most perfect way to pass the weekend. The problem was to get from the little parade ground security gate down the hill to the social hall without the officer in the dock tower seeing us. He could observe almost all of the road that we had to travel if he was looking in that direction. So, one of us would call the officer in the dock tower. As the telephone was on the wall that faced the water, the officer had to look away from the road while he talked. This would give the rest of the kids a chance to make a dash down the road to the social hall and let themselves in through a window. The window had a broken latch, so access was easy. This window was located on the ground floor below street level. The next part of the plan was to help the one who had called the dock tower get down the road to the social hall. A few minutes were allowed to go by, then the phone person would open the gate where he would have a good view of the social hall, but the tower officer could not see him even if he was looking toward the road. As soon as one of the kids at the social hall would wave his hands, it meant that they were calling the dock tower again from the social hall. The last kid would ease out till he could see the tower officer. As soon as the officer answered the phone, the last boy would make a dash down the road to the hall. Over a two year period we must have done this at least twenty times. We would usually go down to the hall in the late afternoon so we could come back after dark without the necessity of any further phone calling. What did we say on the phone to the tower officer? We would ask him things like "I heard there was a special boat running at 4:00 pm today, is that true?" Another line we used was "I am having a friend over next week, what do I have to do?" We also knew who was working in the dock tower before we ever called. Some of the officers had not heard our different lines too many times, and with shift changes and assignments, several different officers worked in the dock tower as was true of other locations.

One day another boy and I went down to the social hall, and while having a relaxing game of pool, we heard a door shut upstairs in the dance hall and kitchen area. We quickly put the pool balls in the pockets, and dashed over to where pins were set up in the bowling alley. We laid flat in the area just behind the pins in the dug out. We heard someone coming down the stairs from

View of the Social Hall or Officers Club. The top floor contained a dance floor which was used for several events. It also contained a projection room and kitchen. The bottom floor contained a two lane bowling alley and two pool tables. Courtesy of Phil Palmer.

the upper level. We were flat on the floor almost afraid to breathe. We waited, but heard nothing for what seemed like an eternity. Then we could hear the footsteps again. This time they seemed like they were headed away. I ventured a look and saw an officer walking towards the door, which leads outside the hall, up some stairs and hopefully out of our lives. Instead he turned and walked to the end of the walkway and stopped. He seemed to be looking down at the water. We figured that he had already checked the upper floor, so we would go upstairs and hide until he left. As quietly as we could, we walked over to the stairs and eased our way up to the upper level. We went into the kitchen and hid in a small pantry located just behind the projection room. We were careful not to close the door all the way as you could not open it from the inside. It also left very little air inside when closed. A few minutes later we heard the officer come back up the stairs and walk into the kitchen. We held our breath as he walked by and pushed the pantry door closed, leaving us virtually locked in. Fortunately the pantry had a light in it. So, when we thought it was safe, I turned it on. We realized at once that there was no silverware in the pantry, as most items like that are locked up because of the inmates. After all, we were inside the security area. My friend tried to use his gate key to slide the latch back, but the key was not long enough. We had just about decided to kick open the door, as it was very thin and made of cheap wood, when I decided to try my comb to slide back the latch. It was a small latch and my comb was one of those long barber types. It was getting awfully stuffy in there. I slipped the comb between the door jam and put pressure on the latch. It slid a little and, as I told my friend to push, I pressed harder. Just as I felt the plastic comb snap, the door popped open. I now had a very short comb in my hand and a slightly longer one on the floor. I picked up the other piece of the comb, and as it was now dark, we ran up the hill and headed for our own houses.

My father came home from work one day about a week after our little escapade with a memo he and all the other officers had received. As he began to read it, I felt my legs grow a little weak. He said that prison authorities knew that teenagers were sneaking down to the social hall on weekends, and, if caught, that they (officials) would close the social hall to dances in the future. He also told me that a recent foot patrol of the area had been initiated. I had found that out

Photograph of the lower floor of the social hall with bowling alley and pool tables. Courtesy of Golden Gate National Recreation Area.

first hand. My father never asked me if I was one of the boys who was going down to the social hall, but he really made me wonder by saying, "You can't say you have not been warned." Our group never again made any unauthorized trips down to the social hall. We almost outsmarted ourselves.

Some of the things we did would not have been off limits in other circumstances. However, all in all, we were a pretty good bunch of kids. Of the eight boys in our group, three became police officers, two are teachers, one a parole agent, one a plant manager, and one a military pilot. Most all of us were in the military. It is interesting to note, however, that not one of the group is in the prison service. I guess we all realized what a demanding job our fathers had on Alcatraz.

Kids did not just loaf around the island all the time. In 1950 I got a part time job working in a gas station on Bay Street in San Francisco. It was located about two miles from the boat dock at Pier 4. My folks would only allow me to work on weekends during school. The two extra phones that were now in use on the island were convenient. I could talk to my girlfriend nights when it was not busy at the gas station. I always closed the station at 11:00 pm and headed for the dock in order to catch the 11:30 boat home. As I said earlier, it was about a two mile walk to the dock, so I would save time by going through a train tunnel which ran under Fort Mason and came out only two blocks from the island's pier. The only time it got a little scary in the tunnel was when a train came through. You had to lay down flat on a two foot wide walkway, close your eyes, and hold your ears until it passed. I have often thought whether or not walking the two miles over the streets would have saved me a few early gray hairs.

During the summer of 1951, I worked as often as possible saving to buy a car. In July I turned sixteen years old and obtained my driver's license. By the end of the summer I had enough money to buy an old 1933 Ford Coupe. It gave me a great deal of freedom to go just about anywhere I wanted. I could take my girlfriend to a show or on a picnic, etc. That first car was a dream come true. It was not much, but it was mine.

All the teenagers on the island enjoyed dancing; however, it was not always easy to get a chaperon. Our group of girls and boys had an alternative plan. We would all go up to the doctor's house and hold a dance. The doctor had two daughters in our age group and were one of the very few families who lived inside the security fence. By this time however, it seemed like all the kids in our group had keys to the security gates.

The doctor's house was very large with a basement which consisted of five rooms. We used the largest room for dancing.

There were several major events on the island, most of which took place at the social hall. There were also many unscheduled events that took place at different times of the year. All island teenagers seemed to roller skate two months out of the year, usually October and April. We also had volley ball games in the handball court. The boys would challenge the girls and spot them up to seven points. Sometimes the games were very close. As I stated before, some of the girls were excellent players.

Scheduled events usually started for teenagers with the Valentines Day dance, held at the social hall. The next event, which was discontinued in the early fifties, was a 4th of July watermelon feed held on the dock between 6:00 pm and 8:00 pm. Everyone was invited to this affair. We all ate watermelon till we thought we were going to explode. By the time the event was over, the dock looked like one big red stain. The mess was cleaned up by the two off-duty officers who would start up the fire truck, "Old Red" and hose off the dock. Fortunately, that is about the only use the truck ever got while I was on the island.

Whenever we needed some firecrackers for the fourth of July, we could always find them in the Chinatown section of San Francisco. After all, it has the second largest Chinese population outside of mainland China. Every year it was the same thing in Chinatown. There was always this guy standing on a corner reading a paper. He was there for eight years that I knew of, and for all I know he may be there still. We would walk up to him and tell him we needed some firecrackers. He would always say "follow me kid", no matter how many of us there were. He would then proceed to take us on a half hour tour of Chinatown. I guess this was to make sure no one was following us. He was so careful, you would think we were asking for a set of blue prints to make an A-bomb. Finally, we entered the back of a small store that was covered with boxes from floor to ceiling. We were shown some samples, made our purchase, then followed the same guy with the paper back to the corner where we knew we could always find him.

As the Chinese New Year was and still is very big in San Francisco, we could always obtain firecrackers in late January. Of course, we had to fire off all the firecrackers before we went back to the island. If you were caught with them on you, heaven only knows what might have happened. They were definitely a no-no on Alcatraz.

The next event that took place on Alcatraz was a Halloween party for children twelve and under. That was on a friday night. As soon as the children's party was over, all the teenagers would rush down to the social hall and put up their decorations for the big Halloween dance, which was held the next night. It was a costume affair and everyone always had a great time.

Of course, the big event of the season on the island was Christmas. As I have mentioned before, there was caroling. This was followed by a Christmas party at the social hall. The party was mainly for pre-teen children. The Chief Lighthouse Keeper was just perfect for the job of Santa Claus. I remember sitting on his lap the first Christmas I spent on the island. The Officers' and Women's Clubs would get together and buy gifts so that everyone of the children who attended would receive a gift from Santa. The Christmas party was the one occasion that brought just about everyone on the island together each year. Except, of course, for the officers who had duty. When the party was over, some of the people would go home and get ready for Midnight Mass. It was celebrated in the solarium, which as I said earlier, was located on top of (C) Building in the new apartments.

The main event for older teenagers at this time of the year though, was the Christmas formal dance. The girls would dress up in evening gowns and the boys would wear tuxedos. Just like any other formal dance, the boy would pick up the girl at her house and bring her a corsage. You may be asking how I managed this as my girl's father was not fond of me. Very simple, I picked her up at a friend's house. From the time I started going with her, there was never a truce between her father and me. Her mother, however, was very nice to me, and that in itself made me feel a little better about everything. Also my mother and Joan's mother were fairly good friends. My mother was also very fond of Joan.

Getting back to the dance, there were also several people that came over from San Francisco for the big affair. It was a little bit of an inconvenience. Anyone who had guests coming over to the island had to notify the authorities days in advance, and then take the boat over to the mainland to meet them. After they were checked in on the island, the guests became the responsibility of the person who brought them. When the dance was over, each person would have to escort their guest down to the dock and make sure they checked out with the dock officer. This was done in time for the guest to catch the 12:15 am boat. This was the last boat to the mainland until the next morning.

New Years Eve on the island was about the same every year. A group of adults would make the rounds of different houses, and there was some drinking. I do believe, however, that most adults, especially the officers, tempered their drinking, as they never knew when something would go wrong up at the prison.

Shortly after the new year of 1952 began, my old car moaned for the last time, and just about died. Now that I was spoiled by having my own car, my number one priority was to quickly replace it. I had a friend drive me around looking at used cars. I thought I had seen all that the world had to offer until I found a nice little 1941 Chevy Club Coupe. It ran and looked like a new car, and I knew that I would have to own it. I gave the man twenty-five dollars to hold it for me. It was at a used car lot. Now I had to get my old car down to the lot and trade it in. That night I told my folks about this great car, and my mother asked me why I could not get the old one fixed. I told her that I thought it had a terminal case of the flu and that it would cost more to fix it than buy the other one. As the next day was saturday, my mother said she would take a ride in both cars to see what we should do. I asked one of my friends to go with me for support. The next day we drove my old car two blocks up the hill from the foot of Van Ness Avenue. By the time we were at the top, the car was shaking and smoking so bad, my mother began to agree with me. So we headed for the used car lot. I took her for a ride in the Chevy and, along with my friend's help, I think we convinced her it was a new Cadillac. Anyway, I got the Chevy and never had a bit of trouble with it, even though the car was eleven years old at the time. It also meant that I could take more friends out with me because of the back seat.

Things went along normally, until June 1952. Sometime during that month, Joan informed me that her father, who had recently been promoted to Associate Warden, was being transferred to McNeil Island in July. I was upset, to say the least. I guess I thought things would go along the way they were forever.

I can remember as though it was only yesterday. My girl left the island on July 14, 1952, just five days before my birthday. I can recall getting up early that morning and going over to her house. I knocked on the door and she came out. We sat on the steps. I can not remember what we talked about, but I am sure it was the same things that have been said for thousands of years in this same situation. Finally, her mother came out and advised us that it was time to go. We said our goodbyes, and left each other vowing that we would write. We did correspond for several months.

I had a little problem being on my own, and I found myself getting somewhat absent minded. I was making a lot of dumb mistakes such as filling up a gas tank at work, when the customer only asked for $2 worth. My boss told me to take a little time off and get my head screwed back on straight. So I took his advise and stayed off about a month, until things looked brighter. I returned and found that things were better. I noted that now customers were getting the right amount of gas for their money, and the boss wasn't watching me quite so closely.

After a while I began dating. I went out with a few different girls, mostly from school. I never went out with any of these girls more than once or twice. The problem goes back to the old one of boat catching. If you missed the 12:15 boat, you were stuck in town until the next day. Things just sort of limped along until one night a friend asked me to come down to the social hall and help hang some decorations for the Halloween dance. I finally agreed. While I was hanging crepe paper all over the place from a ladder, I heard a voice behind me ask if I would like a coke. As I turned around I realized that it was a girl who had moved onto the island a couple of years ago. She was very pretty, but almost a year older than me. I had been going steady nearly the entire time this girl, whom I'll call Susan, had lived on the island, so I only knew her on a casual basis.

Well, as fate would have it, I walked her home that night. As Susan was not going with anyone special at the moment, I asked her to go to the dance with me. One thing led to another, and within a few months we were engaged, but as fate stepped in again, never to marry. Later, being shipped overseas for twenty-five months ended the relationship.

There was one event I have remembered over all the years. During my last summer on the island, our group challenged the officers to a baseball game.

For weeks we were out on the diamond practicing. We felt we could beat them easily. Finally the day of the big game came. It seemed like the officers were getting younger, as some did not look much older than our team. There was such a large crowd on hand, we were wondering who was watching the inmates. People were sitting on the grass in front of both B and C Buildings. The game got underway and for the first inning it looked fairly even. Then this left handed hitter came to bat for their team. He hit the ball so hard that it cleared the cliff wall between C Building and the captain's house on the fly and made it to the water. It must have gone 400 feet. (This officer was the same one who was shot at in the dock tower during the 1946 riot). The next time he came to bat, he did exactly the same thing; only this time a couple of officers were on base. Well, to conclude this painful story, the final score ended officers 17, teenagers 1. I pitched that day, and I recall just about the whole game except for one thing. I have no idea how we ever scored a run. I don't think we ever got over that beating. We took a razzing from everyone for a long time. I believe on that day I decided a baseball career was definitely not in my future. I do not think that baseball suffered because of my decision.

The one thing I loved to do on the island was to fish. When I was younger, we were not allowed to go. But now I was seventeen, and some of my friends and I would get permission on weekends to fish from the dock all night. We were allowed to go down to the dock anytime after 9:00 pm, and we could fish till the next morning as long as we left by 6:00 am. Almost every friday night for the last year I lived on the island, my friends and I would pick up shrimp at a bait shop in San Francisco near the harbor. The only problem was when we would catch the prison launch to the island, we got some fairly upsetting looks from people.

When it was time to go down to the dock, we filled our coffee thermos bottles up and made enough sandwiches to feed an army. We put on our usual two pairs of pants, socks, and jackets. We used to wedge our fishing poles between the dock pilings, put the reel on stardrag, and sit in one of the two pick-up trucks I talked about earlier in regards to prisoner transfers. Sometimes we would talk for hours, then all of a sudden one of the stardrags would begin to whine. We would all jump out of the truck to see who had the fish hooked. If we were fishing way

The writer in his graduation cap and gown. The photograph was taken in our last home on the island which was located in (B) Building. (Picture taken June 9, 1953)

off dock, it would usually mean we had a leopard or sand shark. The sand sharks were tough, but trying to land a leopard shark took a great amount of endurance. The only rest you got was when the shark would sound. We sometimes landed them up to six feet long. We caught several types of fish on the island from the sharks all the way down to the little smelt. It seemed we never got tired of fishing on the island. Since leaving Alcatraz, I have fished several other locations in the world from Florida to the South Pacific. However, catching fish was not only more fun on the island, but the catch was more plentiful.

Well, the spring of 1953 finally arrived, and it was time to graduate from high school. It turned out to be a wonderful evening except for one small thing. My girl and I missed the last boat that night. We were on our way to a party in San Francisco when we got stuck in some mud at the beach. By the time we got the car back on the road, it was so late we had to head straight for the boat dock in order to catch the last boat. As things turned out, we did not make it. Gentleman that I was, though, I had Susan call one of her friends, and she stayed with her that night. I drove back down to the dock and slept in my car.

The next morning I went home on the first boat, and Susan waited to return to the island on the 10:00 am boat. That way we figured gossip would be kept to a minimum. Of course, we were wrong. It seems like too many people were aware that Susan and I would be attending my graduation that evening. Naturally, people would assume we would go to a few parties. But who was going to believe we got stuck in the mud? Anyway, the minute I stepped through my front door, the phone began ringing. At 7:00 am on a saturday morning, it did not take a whiz kid to figure out who was calling. I picked up the phone, and sure enough it was Susan's father wondering what had happened. I explained our unfortunate set of circumstances to the best of my ability. I don't believe, though, he was convinced. As I hung up the phone, I looked at it and said half out loud, "This is going to be my future father-in-law?" As fate would have it the phone woke my mother, and she got up to see what was happening. There I was sitting on the bed taking my shoes off when she walked into my bedroom. Again I explained what had transpired. She advised me to meet the 10:00 am boat when it arrived, escort Susan home, and explain the circumstances to her parents in person. Somehow knowing that this was the right thing to do did not make it any easier. Although Susan's parents appeared somewhat satisfied with our explanation, it was several days before our friends quit making jokes about the incident.

There always seemed to be a mystical illusion about one phase of living on the island. It always seemed to me, as I am sure it did to others, that as soon as you stepped onto the island boat and headed for Alcatraz, you felt safe from the outside world. This must sound strange to the reader to say that going to where a maximum security prison was located made one feel safe. It is very hard to explain, but I do know that as the years went by and I spent more time in the city, this illusion began to fade.

In August, 1953, my father had decided to retire effective October 12 of the same year. I cannot say I was happy about this turn of events, but I realized that as one door of my life was closing, another one was just beginning to open up.

After my father had made his plans known, I joined the United States Coast Guard. I asked them if they could make my activation effective October 15, 1953.

The night before we moved from the island, my friends gave me a farewell dance at the social hall. The next day as my family walked from the dock house to the prison launch for the last time, I looked back towards the balcony. There some of my friends waved to me. I then looked up to the window where my fiancee lived. She threw me a kiss. After doing the same back, I stepped onto the boat, found a seat in the cabin, and got ready for my last trip from the island.

As I sat there and thought about so many, many things, something suddenly dawned on me. This illusion of safety was now gone. From this point on, that outside world at the other end of this boat trip would now be my only world. During the ride over, several passengers on the boat wished my family well. When the boat docked at Pier 4, many of them helped us unload our furniture and house items.

As the boat headed back towards the island, I watched it for a long time. Could it have been eleven years since we took that first boat ride to Alcatraz? A few minutes later my father, who had gone to get the car, drove down the dock and stopped next to our household goods. We loaded the car and drove off the dock. I turned and looked out the back window of the car at my home of so many wonderful years. I said goodbye under my breath.

I now realized that the time had finally come for me to look to the future and get on with my life.

EIGHT

A Final Visit—1966

It had been thirteen years since my father retired from the Federal Prison Service. Many things had changed in my life since then as they had with my former home on Alcatraz. After leaving the island I served four years with the U.S. Coast Guard. While still in the service, I married and began to raise a family. After two years of working and going to school, I launched my career in the field of law enforcement. I had dreamed of this since I was a little boy. I began my career with the State of California in 1961. In 1965 I applied for and was accepted by a city in Southern California. My father had passed away in 1964.

By 1966 I had decided to take my family—wife Gwen and two children Don Jr., eight years old, and Tricia, seven years old—for a trip to Alcatraz Island. I made this decision so that my children, who knew very little about their grandfather, would get a chance to see where he had worked, and to give them a sense of what he was all about. The other reason, of course, was that my children could see where their father had spent so many of his childhood years.

In 1963 when Alcatraz was closed as a federal prison, it was turned over to the U.S. General Service Department. The man who retired and became caretaker of the island was the father of one of my friends whom I'll call Gary, and who I shared many good years with on "The Rock." Except for the caretaker the island was now deserted.

I got in touch with Gary and asked if I could bring my family over to the island for a couple of days visit. He said that he would be glad to see me. So when I told my family of the plan, they were very excited. I too must confess that the

One of two security dogs that had the run of the dock in order to keep would-be trespassers away from the island. It appears that the dog in the house is resting after a hard nights patrol. Courtesy John "Bud" Hart.

thought of returning to the island after all these years to have a look around excited me also.

The reader will remember that I said dependents were allowed on less than one third of the twelve acre island. The visit then, would allow me to explore the entire area. I knew I would feel like a kid in a candy store. In April we made the drive to San Francisco where I contacted my friend. The next morning he and his father made the trip from the island in a small cabin cruiser, which they used to run back and forth to the city for supplies. After exchanging greetings, we boarded the boat and headed for the island. I found myself almost as excited as the first time I took that boat ride to Alcatraz so many years ago now. (24 years)

When we arrived at the island and disembarked, I was astonished to say the least. If looking around the dock area was any indication of how unchanged the island had remained, then this trip would be very worthwhile. It was deserted except for us. There was no dock tower officer, dock officer or anyone else. The second thing I noticed right away was that there were two large dogs who had the run of the entire dock area. I was told that the dogs were to keep trespassers away from the island. One glance at either of these two animals would convice just about anyone to stay away. I must admit though that it sure seemed strange not only to see dogs on Alcatraz, but also to watch them running loose. As I thought back to my childhood days and the "no dog rule" on the island, a slight smile came to the corners of my mouth. We rode up to the big parade ground in one of the old prison vehicles. We stopped at C Building where my friend's father had taken over the three ground floor apartments for living guarters, one of which was my old home. We had some breakfast and then my friend took us on a tour of the prison and all the other buildings "up top." As I said before, just the thought of having the run of the place made me very excited and brought back the little boy in me.

Before going inside the prison, my family and I took a tour of the chief medical officer's and warden's homes. It felt odd walking through the now empty rooms. As I stood there at one of the large living room windows, a wave of nostalgia washed over me. The window gave such a commanding view of most of the residences on the island. It was a rare spring day on the island, and you could see

San Francisco and the Bay Bridge. Standing there I must have day dreamed myself back in time. It was hard to believe that it had been thirteen years since my father had retired and we said goodbye to all our friends and moved from the island.

I was brought back to the present by my little boy pulling on my sleeve and saying, "Let's see the prison, daddy." I smiled, took his hand and we walked the few yards to the prison's main entrance. We walked through all the administration offices and eventually entered the main cell house. In all my years on the island, this was my first visit to the heart of the prison itself. Of course I knew the entire layout of the cell house as my father had told my brother and me about it many times. I found myself eagerly exploring the various cell blocks and the cells. It was an eerie feeling walking through this now deserted cell house where so many men were forced by prison rules and regulations to literally march to the tune of a strict taskmaster, the federal prison system.

We continued our tour by walking through the prison dining room and kitchen area. I told my children that their grandfather had worked in just about all the prison assignments many times. I took my children over to the "dark cells" or "hot box" cells as they had been called by the inmates. I told them what they were used for and then asked if they wanted to be locked up in one of them. They both said they would, so I put them in the same cell and shut the door. Within fifteen seconds they both wanted out. I could see that this was not their idea of fun. After taking a look at the prison yard, Gary showed us the cells where the Anglin brothers and Frank Morris made their bid for freedom less than four years before by chipping out the vents to the rear of their cells. We also took a look at the west gun gallery where the riot of 1946 had begun. Other than the empty cells and the unwaxed floors, it appeared that the cell house could have been in use the day before.

Gary had fixed up a cell for display to show how one looked when someone had occupied it. There was a mattress on the cot with a folded blanket at one end. All the toilet products were there as were a pair of slippers, a calendar, and guitar. While standing there in the corridor and looking into that cell, I wondered just what kind of a man had occupied it. I glanced at the bunk and thought how many times did this inmate wake up in the middle of the night in a cold sweat and wonder where he had misplaced his hopes and dreams.

That afternoon while my children, who were worn out from the trip, were taking a nap, my friend and I decided to do some more exploring. We first headed for the social hall. As we walked down the hill from the little parade ground, we recalled how we use to sneak down to the hall during the day in order to shoot pool. I remembered all the calls to the dock tower to distract the officer. As we walked on I glanced around and looked at the tower. It seemed strange somehow that it was now empty. My father had put in his share of shifts in that tower.

When we arrived and entered the top floor, I was amazed to find that the kitchen, projector room, and the dance floor area looked nice enough to have been used the night before. I asked my friend if he would like to shoot a game of pool and maybe even bowl a line. We played a game of pool and bowled a line each. He set the pins for me one game and I set the pins for him the next game. As I was setting pins I remembered how I used to make 35 cents a line on friday and saturday nights for some of the younger married officers on the island. After leaving the social hall we took a walk down to the dock. The dogs paid little attention to me. We walked around the dock awhile and then I suggested we climb the dock tower. This was to fulfill one of my childhood dreams. It was easy to see why the dock tower was placed exactly where it was, as it allowed a commanding view of the dock, the boat docking area, and the road which leads to the dock. During its prison days, this tower would also afford the officer the opportunity of scanning most of the east side of the island. He could, with binoculars check the cliffs for anything unusual, while at the same time see to it that no unauthorized boats came within the two hundred yard limit of the island.

While standing there leaning against the rail of the catwalk which leads around the outside of the tower, Gary and I spoke of the many nights we spent fishing off the dock until the sunrise forced us to pack up our fishing gear and head for home. It seemed so peaceful and quiet there looking out over the now deserted dock. There were no children talking or laughing as they disembarked from the after school launch. As the sun was beginning to drop low in the western sky, we decided to take a walk around the beach before we called it a day. After we had walked around the southeast end of the island, we began to climb up the path which led to the big parade ground. About fifty feet up the path, we came to the large billboard sign which read "Cable Crossing Do Not Anchor."

A picture of the unmanned dock tower. It seemed strange now to see it empty. My father put in his share of shifts in that tower. Courtesy of John "Bud" Hart.

Just for a moment in my mind, I returned to a time over twenty years earlier when after being on the beach we would hide behind the sign, so the island launch could not see us as it made its trip to San Francisco. Gary interrupted my daydream and told me it was about dinner time, and we had better get back before someone thought we were lost. I laughed and said that I did not think there was one chance in a million that either one of us could get lost on Alcatraz Island. As we headed across the big parade ground, I vowed to myself that I would get up early the next day and explore as much of my old home as was humanly possible.

When we arrived at our host's apartment, my wife told me my son was running a fever, and that we might have to leave earlier than planned and drive home. Of course, I felt bad about cutting the trip short, but we agreed that if my son was not better by noon the next day, we would leave.

Sleeping that night was all but impossible. I hoped that my son would feel better in the morning, so we could stay until late afternoon before heading back to Los Angeles. The next morning I was awake before dawn. I got up and checked to see if my son's fever had gone down. It appeared it had, so I got dressed and went to the kitchen to have some breakfast. I planned to make one last trip around the island to places I had not seen the day before. As I sat there eating my cereal and looking out over the big parade ground, I thought about all the wonderful experiences I had as a child living on the island.

My daughter walked into the kitchen and asked me what I was doing. I told her I was going to make one last trip around the island and she could go with me. Her eyes lit up as she ran to get dressed. A couple of minutes later she reappeared and said that she was ready to go. I made her eat some cereal first, and after leaving a note, we left on our little exploration.

We first went to the handball court (gym). There was no lock on the door. I told my daughter that the gym was where we played basketball, volleyball, and table tennis. When we left the gym, I pointed out where we use to spend so much time roller skating. She asked me if I had liked living on the island. I told her I had liked it very much, as did almost all the kids who grew up on Alcatraz. I told her that next I was going to show her the first two places where I had lived after moving to the island. We walked down to the lower balcony of

111

64 Building and entered the now completely empty apartment. (same location as picture of me in the sailor suit) We walked out the back door and onto the steel bars that formed a canopy over an old narrow road built by the army in 1866. The narrow road/walkway ran the entire length of the westside of 64 Building and along its way were several old rooms including the bomb shelter where so many years before we had our little fire. As I said before, everyone on the island called the semi-tunnel "Chinatown."

Standing there just outside my old back door, I remembered the time my mother had thrown some of my old, war-time canvas tennis shoes into the trash can next to the door. She said they were all worn out. I had sneaked out just after dark and retrieved them. I must have worn those shoes another six months, much to the dismay of my mother.

My daughter and I wandered around the island for another hour. At the north end of the upper balcony, one is about fifty feet directly across from the dock tower, and at just about the same height. I told my daughter that her grandfather had worked many times in the tower. After explaining just what the duties of the dock tower officer were, I said it was time to get back and see how her brother was doing. On the way back to my friend's place we made a side trip to visit the cottages, which were located at the southeast corner of the parade ground. Even though the six cottages were constructed of wood, they were in remarkably good repair except for some minor paint chips on the exterior. We then walked over to the captain's and associate warden's place. Both apartments appeared to be in excellent shape and the carpeting was still in both. It looked as if the people who had lived there had just moved out the day before.

We then returned to my friend's house, and my wife advised we would have to leave as my boy's temperature was up again. As much as I hated to leave, I knew that the time had come to once again say goodbye to my old home.

We packed our bags and said our goodbyes. My friend's father drove us down to the dock, where we boarded his little cabin cruiser that transported us back to the mainland. As I walked over to where I had parked the car, I had the strangest feeling that the island would not remain much longer the way I had just seen it.

The island stayed fairly intact until November of 1969, when several American Indians took possession of the island and claimed it as a part of an earlier treaty made with the United States. After eighteen months of occupation, the Federal Marshals and the U.S. Coast Guard removed the remaining Indians from the island. During this period five buildings were gutted by fire. Another four were eventually razed by the government due to damage to plumbing, etc., and ten years of standing idle. The only thing I know for certain is what made the island magical for me was now gone. I knew after hearing about the damage and that buildings had been torn down, I could never return to the same Alcatraz Island I had left so long ago. However, nothing can ever erase from my mind those wonderful—boyhood memories.

THE WARDENS OF ALCATRAZ

James A. Johnston 1934-1948

Edwin Swope 1948-1955

Paul J. Madigan 1955-1961

Olin Blackwell 1961-1963

114

NINE

A Study In Pictures—History Preserved

After writing about the various locations on Alcatraz Island, it would not seem right to end this book without allowing the reader a chance to view some of the places, buildings, and structures that have been referred to. One can no longer visit the former federal penitentiary and photograph all the buildings and structures I have written about.

Example: The only free standing tower still intact is the dock tower, and it, too, is in disrepair.

Anyone who visits the island must realize that there have been no repairs made to the buildings or structures for almost a quarter of a century. There are a couple of exceptions to this. Two movies have been made on the island in recent years. The first in 1979 concerning the Morris and Anglin's escape attempt, the movie company had to refurbish much of the prison's interior to a point where it would appear authentic as a working prison. There was also a partial metal roof put on 64 Building. The National Park Service, which gives tours and has control of the island is at present utilizing voluntary help in an attempt to restore some of the areas of the island, so more of it can be opened to the public. The National Park Service hosts nearly one million visitors each year.

Some of the photographs you will view on the next several pages have never been published. All but a few of the photographs were taken while Alcatraz was an active Federal Penitentiary.*

---

* In order to see where certain buildings, structures, and locations on the island were and are, please refer to sketch map on page 139.

115

Anyone can see this United States Government emblem which is mounted just above the entrance leading to the prison administration offices. Courtesy of Golden Gate National Recreation Area.

The warden's office located in the north/east corner of the administration building, which is a part of the main prison building. The four wardens of Alcatraz (Warden Johnston, Warden Swope, Warden Madigan, and Warden Blackwell) all used this office. Courtesy of Golden Gate National Recreation Area.

Over-all view of the south portion of "The Rock." This photograph gives an excellent view of living quarters on the island. Starting counter clockwise from the lighthouse there is the bachelor quarters (bldg. A), the new apartment building (bldg. B & C), the Captain's & Associate Warden's apartments, the cottages or bungalows, 64 Building, and back up to the warden's house which is adjacent to the lighthouse. Courtesy of San Francisco Public Library.

The United States Coast Guard Lighthouse Station on Alcatraz. The lighthouse in this photograph was constructed in 1909. The attached houseing facilities could accomodate three families. The lighthouse and housing was almost completely destroyed by fire in 1970 during the Indian occupation of the island. Courtesy of Golden Gate National Recreation Area.

One of two cell blocks in C section which clearly show the three tiers of cells. Cells could be opened individually or a whole row on the same tier could be opened all at once. Courtesy of Golden Gate National Recreation Area.

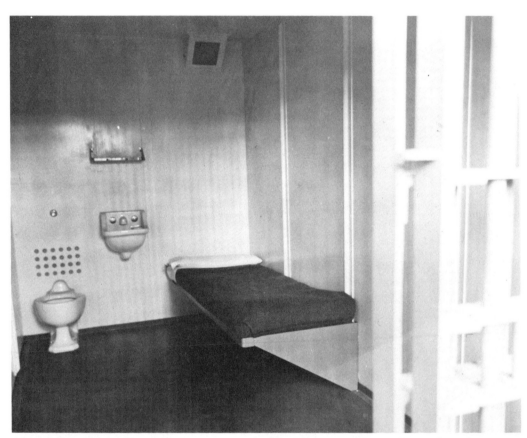

A view of a solitary confinement cell located in (D) Block. Inmates in these cells were locked up all the time or until prison authorities decided they could join the general prison population. The cells were about twenty five percent larger than the cells in (B) and (C) Block. Courtesy of Golden Gate National Recreation Area.

An officer keeps a lonely vigil at night in the cell house between (B) and (C) Cell Blocks. This main corridor was called "Broadway" by the inmates. All the floors in the cell house were kept in a highly polished state. Courtesy of Golden Gate National Recreation Area.

Photograph of stairway leading from the lower balcony of 64 building to the dock area. The photo gives a good view of the dock watch tower. The tower was built to replace a smaller tower which had a cat-walk that connected it to the upper balcony. It is one of the highest free-standing towers ever built (1939-40). Courtesy of San Francisco Public Library.

Photograph of west side of the island looking north. In the foreground is the prison yard with the catwalk running to the road tower. At the end of the yard is a gun cage and beyond the hill tower, to the left, is the west industry building with the tower on the roof. Courtesy of John "Bud" Hart.

An officer on duty in the west road tower. This tower was separated from the prison yard by the gate which is completely surrounded by barbedwire. The catwalk allowed the officer to walk directly to the south/west corner of the yard. Courtesy of Golden Gate National Recreation Area.

This is a view of the entire west side of the island as seen from San Francisco. Although this photograph could have been taken anytime from 1940 (year (A), (B) and (C) Buildings completed) through 1969, it would be impossible to capture on film the shot today. With the exception of the lighthouse tower, all the other buildings to the south/east are gone. Fortunately, Alcatraz Island's main attraction, the prison itself, is still intact. Courtesy Golden Gate National Recreation Area.

This photograph is of the warden's house. As one can see it was a three story structure that consisted of seven bedrooms and four bathrooms. It was originally built in the late 1920's for the Army Post Commander prior to Alcatraz becoming a Federal Prison. The house was completely destroyed by fire during the Indian occupation in 1970. Courtesy of Golden Gate National Recreation Area.

This picture is of the Chief Medical Officer's house. It was a two story structure, however, there was a large basement which consisted of five rooms. On several occasions your writer would join other teenagers for dances in the largest of these basement rooms. This stately house was located directly behind the Warden's house, and it too was destroyed by fire during the Indian occupation in 1970. Courtesy of Golden Gate National Recreation Area.

The Captain and Associate Warden's apartments. Both sides had two stories and basements. Building was torn down by the General Service Administration in the early 1970's. Courtesy of Golden Gate National Recreation Area.

A photograph of one of four cottages or bungalows which allowed residences for six families. They were also torn down at the same time the above apartment building was demolished. Courtesy of Golden Gate National Recreation Area.

Photograph taken on the east side of the island approaching the dock. Notice the social hall just to the right with the tunnel/pistol range ahead and the dock tower in the distance. Courtesy of John "Bud" Hart.

*View of the handball court—located on the big parade ground. The warden's house and lighthouse over-
looks the area from above. Just to the right of the gym (woman walking) was the roller skating area.
To the far right is the south/west end of 64 Building, which housed the old post office. The apartment
just below the chimney was my home from 1944–47. Gentleman to left is a friends grandfather. Picture
taken facing north in 1939. Note security fence behind gym. Courtesy of Edward Faulk.*

This structure was known as (B) Building or the new apartments. It was actually a part of (C) Building. The total unit of (B) and (C) comprised nineteen apartments (counting a roof apartment), and were modern in every respect. My family lived in the bottom left apartment in the early 1950's. Rent was $42.50 for the two bedroom apartment. Courtesy of Golden Gate National Recreation Area.

"Alcatraz in Bloom"—even though the prison was closed when this picture was taken it appears, that nothing can keep the wild flowers from blooming. Photograph was taken near the laundry building looking in a north/west direction towards the islands' industry section. Courtesy of John "Bud" Hart.

A view of old 64 building which faces the little parade ground. The front side faces the dock. This building was built by the Army in 1905 and is still standing. My family lived in this building for four years. Courtesy of Golden Gate National Recreation Area.

View along north/east end of island. From left to right is the old tunnel building (which contained the prison pistol range), the social hall, and a couple of industry buildings. Photograph was taken from a plane. Notice the undertow current of the water adjacent to the island. Courtesy of Golden Gate National Recreation Area.

View from the dock house looking north towards the tunnel building—road eventually leads to the prison. Note the stairs at right leading to lower balcony of 64 building and the dock tower at extreme right. Courtesy of Golden Gate National Recreation Area.

View of about ¾ of the east side of the island. It includes 64 building overlooking the dock, the dock tower, tunnel building, storage building and social hall. The prison at the center of the island dominates everything. San Francisco in the background as it looked several years ago. Courtesy of Golden Gate National Recreation Area.

This view is of the north/west end of the island. It includes all of the industry shop area and was where most all of the attempted escapes occurred during the early years that the prison was in operation. The area was completely fenced and barbewired. Notice the fog horn on the extreme tip of the island. Courtesy of Golden Gate National Recreation Area.

This is an excellent photograph of "The Rock." The picture was taken looking in a south/east direction. It gives a good view of the prison and prison yard. This shot is also the only one this writer knows of that shows all three free standing towers: the road tower just off the prison yard (upper right), the hill tower with its long catwalk (lower left), and the dock tower just over the top of the water tower and to the left. Notice the social hall building to the left of the water tower. Courtesy of Golden Gate Recreation Area.

Alcatraz Island Federal Penitentiary (1934–1963)

1 – Prison (with tower on roof)
2 – Prison Kitchen & Dining Room
3 – Prison Yard
4 – Warden's House
5 – Doctor's House
6 – Light House (Coast Guard)
7 – Hill Tower
8 – Water Tower
9 – Dock Tower
10 – Prison Launch Slip
11 – Dock
12 – Dock Office
13 – Electric Gate To Dock
14 – Canteen (Store)
15 – Post Office
16 – "Old 64 Building" (Residential Quarters)
17 – Pistol Range
18 – Storage
19 – Old Social Hall
20 – Prison Industry Building
21 – Power House
22 – Industry Building (with tower on roof)
23 – Industry Building
24 – West Tower
25 – Bachelor Quarters ("A" Building)
26 – Residential Family Quarters ("B" Building)
27 – Residential Family Quarters ("C" Building)
28 – Hand Ball Court (gym)
29 – Captain & Associate Warden's Apartments
30 – Large Parade Ground
31 – Path To Beach
32 – Residential Family Quarters (Cottages)
33 – Little Parade Ground
34 – Beach (Fishing Area)
35 – Security Fence
36 – Fog Horn

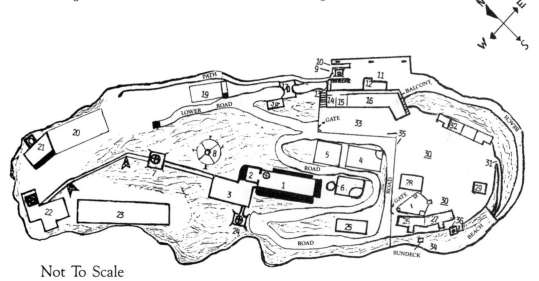

Not To Scale

Officer Charles G. Hurley, Alcatraz Island 1942–1953. Courtesy of Phil Dollison.

A TRIBUTE

The Officers Of Alcatraz

To end this book without an acknowledgment of the officers who served on "The Rock" during its twenty-nine year history, would be to leave part of my story untold. As I said in an earlier chapter, the prison averaged roughly two hundred and eighty inmates incarcerated at any given time on the island. The officers numbered roughly ninety, or about one officer for every 3.1 inmates. It was the highest ratio in the federal prison system. The reason for this, as I have said before, is that these men (inmates) were incorrigible at other federal prisons and that was how they ended up at Alcatraz.

It took a very special kind of officer to supervise this type of inmate. Officers were well aware of the fact that when an inmate was transferred to Alcatraz, his morale would be at an all time low. The officers also knew that after a period the new inmate would become anxious, depressed, and even despondent. This would often lead to frustration and even desperation on the part of the inmate. These traits did not occur with all the newly arrived inmates, but officers were always on the lookout for them. My father kept a record of every inmate who served time on Alcatraz Island during his employment there. He noted name, age, cell number, length of sentence, time served, and his observations about the inmate. He always kept his information current.

It took a well trained officer to recognize any changes in the character traits or moods of the inmates. This is not to imply that officers on Alcatraz were psychologists. For the most part, these officers became experts at observing and handling the behaviors of confined men. The key word here is confined. Another point that should be made here is that just about every officer who worked on

"The Rock" had previous experience at one or more other federal prisons. By and large, the officers who served on the island were a dedicated breed of men who knew their jobs and did them with efficiency and fairness.

My brother and I sitting on a bench that overlooks San Francisco Bay. The bench is still there, but the boys have long since gone. (Picture taken in 1942)

BIBLIOGRAPHY

BOOKS

Campbell, Bruce J., *A Farewell to the Rock. Escape Alcatraz*. New York: McGraw-Hill Book Company, 1963.

Clark, Howard. *Six Against The Rock*. New York: A Jova HB Book 1977.

De Nevi, Don/Bergen, Philip, *Alcatraz 46, The Anatomy of a Classic Prison Tragedy*, San Rafael: Leswing Press, 1974.

Johnston, James A., *Alcatraz Island Prison—And the Men Who Live There*, New York: Charles Seribner's. 1949.

Odier, Pierre. The *Rock—A History of Alcatraz. The Fort/The Prison*. Eagle Rock: L'Image Odier. 1982.

Denis, Alherta, *Spanish Alta California*. MacMillan. 1927.

Engineers at the Golden Gate: U.S. Army Corps of Engineers—San Francisco District, 1980.

Lewis, Emanuel Raymond. *Seacoast Fortifications of the United States: An Introductory History*. Washington: Smithsonian Institution Press, 1970.

Shanks, Jr., Ralph C. *Lighthouses of San Francisco Bay*. San Anselmo: Costano Books. 1976.

Treutlein, Theodore E., *Discovery and Colonization 1769-1776*. California Historical Society. 1968.

Who Discovered San Francisco Bay. San Mateo County Historical Association. 1966

INDEX

148

ACKNOWLEDGMENTS

Without the assistance of the following people and organizations, this book could not have been possible.

Alcatraz Alumni Association
(several individual members)
Chuck Hurley
Gwen Hurley
Bob Orr
Carol Prziborowski
San Francisco Public Library
Sonoma County Library System
U.S. National Parks Service

Photographs
AP/Wide World Photos, Inc.
Phil Dollison
Edward Faulk
Golden Gate National Recreation Area
John "Bud" Hart
Don Hurley Jr.
National Maritime Museum
Phil Palmer
Tricia (Hurley) Rezendes

A Special thanks to:
Kit Close   Esther Faulk
John Martini   Donna Middlemist

FOR ADDITIONAL BOOKS
Send check/money order for $8.49 ea.,
plus shipping/handling of $1.50 to:

Fog Bell Enterprises
P.O. Box 1376
Sonoma, CA 95476
(California residents add $.51 sales tax.)

This Book Makes A Great Gift
Order two or more books, we pay <u>ALL</u> postage.